C0-ATR-977

The Corporate Triangle

The Corporate Triangle

The Structure and Performance of Corporate Systems in a Global Economy

William Lazonick, Ronald Dore and Henk W. de Jong

Edited by

P. H. ADMIRAAL

Copyright © Blackwell Publishers Ltd, 1997

First published 1997

First published in USA 1997
2 4 6 8 10 9 7 5 3 1

Blackwell Publishers Ltd
108 Cowley Road
Oxford OX4 1JF
UK

Blackwell Publishers Inc.
350 Main Street
Malden, Massachusetts 02148
USA

All rights reserved. Except for the quotation of short passages for the
purposes of criticism and review, no part of this publication may be
reproduced, stored in a retrieval system, or transmitted, in any form or
by any means, electronic, mechanical, photocopying, recording or
otherwise, without the prior permission of the publisher.

Except in the United States of America, this book is sold subject to the
condition that it shall not, by way of trade or otherwise, be lent, re-sold,
hired out, or otherwise circulated without the publisher's prior consent in
any form of binding or cover other than that in which it is published and
without a similar condition including this condition being imposed on the
subsequent purchaser.

British Library Cataloguing in Publication Data
A CIP catalogue record for this book is available from the British
Library.

Library of Congress Cataloging in Publication Data

Library of Congress data has been applied for.

ISBN 0-631-207155

Typeset in 11 on 13 pt Garamond
by Ace Filmsetting Ltd, Frome, Somerset.
Printed in Great Britain by Hartnolls Ltd, Bodmin, Cornwall.

This book is printed on acid-free paper.

Contents

Notes on the Contributors

The Editor

Piet Hein Admiraal teaches at the Erasmus University in Rotterdam. He has written several papers and articles about economic systems and industrial organization. In his research he has tried to characterize the market as an economic institution.

The Contributors

William Lazonick started his career as a member of the research team of Alfred Chandler Jr. Nowadays he is working in the Center for Industrial Competitiveness, University of Massachusetts, Lowell. He is the author of a series of publications. The most well-known is his book *Business Organization and the Myth of the Market Economy*, Cambridge University Press, 1991.

Ronald Dore is professor of Economics in London and Bologna. While living in Japan he gathered the information for his famous book *British Factory – Japanese Factory: The Origins of National Diversity in Industrial Relations*, University of California Press, 1973 (2nd ed. 1990).

Henk de Jong is a leading Dutch economist in the field of industrial organization. The focus of his work is on the dynamic aspects of economic life. His most important book has been translated into English under the title *Dynamic Market Theory*. Also he is the editor of *The Structure of European Industry*, Kluwer, Deventer, 1989.

Preface

In this volume you will find three essays based on the traditional F. de Vries-lectures, held in Rotterdam in the autumn of 1995. The first author, William Lazonick, describes the history of the Anglo-Saxon corporate system. Then Ronald Dore contrasts the Japanese firms with their counterparts in the West. In the last chapter Henk de Jong gives a detailed account of the development and the diversity of the continental European corporation.

An interesting theoretical question casts a shadow over all three essays. What is the nature of a corporation? The contributors are struggling in their answer with the standard theoretical concepts. They give a plea for more attention to be paid to the value-creating function of the firm and, in connection with it, to the question of how the corporation is embedded in society.

The lectures are clearly dealing with a subject of crucial importance for the future of our economic and social order. For this reason the F. de Vries Foundation is particularly pleased to present these thought-provoking essays, the more so as they are concerned with a problem in which the eminent economist to whose memory these lectures are dedicated was deeply interested.

P. H. Admiraal

1

The Anglo-Saxon Corporate System

William Lazonick

Organization and Market in Corporate Systems

Faced with the rise of the Asian economies, many Westerners have recently begun to question the adequacy of the organization of their own economies for competing in global markets and sustaining prosperity. There is much to learn through comparative analyses of how different corporate systems contribute to international competitive advantage and sustained economic growth. Given its importance, far too little serious research has been done on today's topic, 'the structure and performance of corporate systems in a global economy'.

We are fortunate to have as one of the speakers today a man who pioneered in the in-depth comparative analysis of corporate systems. In 1973 Ronald Dore published *British Factory – Japanese Factory: The Origins of National Diversity in Industrial Relations*, a book that compared the organization of production in two British plants of the English Electric Company and two Japanese plants of the Hitachi Company (Dore, 1973). Based on field research done at the end of the 1960s, Professor Dore's contribution appeared just as Western observers were becoming

This lecture reflects joint work with Mary O'Sullivan, whose comments I gratefully acknowledge.

[1]

aware of the so-called Japanese 'miracle'. The conventional wisdom up to that time was that, laden with such non-market institutions as permanent employment, collective bonuses and seniority-based pay, the Japanese system fostered inefficiency (see Abbeglen, 1958). Even during the 1970s most Westerners attributed Japan's competitive successes in consumer electronics and automobiles not to superior productive capability but to a willingness of its people to work long hours for relatively low pay.

In contrast to the prevailing view of the inevitable superiority of 'market-oriented' corporate systems, *British Factory – Japanese Factory* explained the economic rationale of the Japanese 'organization-oriented' employment practices while recognizing the distinctive cultural underpinnings of the Japanese model. By relating the comparative case studies of Hitachi and English Electric to the historical development of Japanese and British industry, Professor Dore made a compelling argument that the market-orientation of employment in British enterprises and the organization orientation of Japanese enterprises each made economic sense given the national institutional environment in which these enterprises operated.

The critical difference that Professor Dore found between the two systems was that English Electric bought skills that were readily available on the market at a going price while Hitachi bought the 'capacity to acquire skills' – that is, to develop the productive capabilities of its employees, including its blue-collar workers (although much more so in the case of men than of women) (Dore 1973, pp. 110–11). Writing in the early 1970s, Professor Dore did not put forward the Japanese approach as a model for competitive advantage that could or should be emulated by Britain or other developed economies. But the reader of *British Factory – Japanese Factory* cannot help but get the impression that the organization-oriented Hitachi was a dynamic enterprise and the market-oriented English Electric a stagnant one (see Dore, 1990, Afterword).

[2]

In carrying out his comparative case study, Professor Dore was less concerned with the analysis of global competitive advantage and the lessons for Britain than with the implications of Japan's organization-oriented success for 'late developing' nations. His message to these nations was that industrial development need not, and probably could not, rely on markets to co-ordinate employment relations. Moreover, once an organization-oriented development process had achieved success – relative to a nation's own past even if not in global competition – there was no reason to believe that further progress would require convergence to the market-oriented model.

Given the entrenched belief of most Westerners in the efficiency of the market, however, arguments about an alternative to the market-oriented corporate system faced a hard sell. As Ronald Dore remarked towards the close of his book: 'The majority of economists on whom I have tried these ideas appear very reluctant to give up their assumption that the British market-oriented system is somehow 'normal' and the Japanese a curious deviation to be ascribed wholly to very special 'cultural factors' (Dore 1973, p. 418). According to this market-oriented ideology, no matter what might have worked for Japan in the past, if Japanese industry hoped to compete on global markets in the future Japanese enterprises would have to purge themselves of their organization-oriented relations. If there was a model of social organization relevant for late-developing nations, the market-oriented economists argued, it was to be found in the market-oriented successes of the advanced economies of the West.

The market-oriented economists could not have been more wrong. From the perspective of the 1990s we know that the organization-oriented Japanese model has not withered away in open competition with the market-oriented Western model. Far from Japanese employment practices converging on those prevalent in Britain, for the past 10–15 years enterprises in

[3]

Britain have been furiously trying to become 'Japanese'. Beginning with the Ford Motor Company's unsuccessful 'After Japan' programme for introducing quality circles on the shop floor in Britain, the attention of British industrialists and business academics turned to the possibilities of 'Japanization' (Oliver and Wilkinson, 1992; Strange, 1993). The pressures of global competition, including large-scale direct investments by leading Japanese companies within Britain, finally forced many British industrial employers to recognize that the future lay with the organization-oriented Japanese model. The spread of the so-called Japanese miracle to many other nations in Asia, moreover, suggests that Professor Dore was right about the importance of the organization-oriented model to late developers (see World Bank, 1992; Amsden, 1989; Wade, 1990) – which is why, I suppose, his charge today is to speak about the Asian, rather than just the Japanese, corporate system. My own task, set for me by the De Vries Lecture organizers, is to talk about the structure and performance of the Anglo-Saxon corporate system in the global economy. Epitomized by the corporate systems that currently prevail in Britain and the United States, the Anglo-Saxon (or Anglo-American) system is the most market oriented of the corporate systems that we will be discussing today (see De Jong, 1994). Yet, in terms of the evolution of the structure and performance attributes of corporate systems – for understanding why and under what conditions organization-oriented systems outperform market-oriented systems in global competition – there are important differences between the United States and Britain.

In historical perspective, compared with Britain the American corporate system has been over the course of the twentieth century far more organization-oriented, particularly in terms of its relations with managerial personnel and its control over financial resources for industrial investment (Lazonick, 1991, ch. 1). This organization orientation – manifested in what has been called 'the managerial revolution in American business' (Chandler, 1977) – is, moreover, a prime reason why US enterprises and the US economy have persistently outperformed their British counterparts during this century. Indeed, I have argued that the social foundations of American economic leadership in the twentieth century represented a highly organization-oriented precursor to the Japanese corporate system, with the distinction that in the American case 'the capacity to acquire skills' was confined to those employed within the managerial structure and not extended to those employed on the shop floor (Lazonick, 1991, ch. 1). Furthermore, historical analysis of global competition over the past century shows that the persistent dependence of the British economy and its indigenous enterprises on market-oriented relations is a curious relic of the nineteenth century that must give way to an organization-oriented corporate system if British industry hopes to compete globally with high living standards in the late twentieth century and beyond (see Elbaum and Lazonick, 1986; Lazonick, 1990, ch. 10; and Lazonick, 1991, ch. 1). Why, in contrast to the ideology of market efficiency that pervades Western economics, has the elaboration of an organization-oriented corporate system become ever more important for competitive advantage and sustained economic growth? A growing body of research reveals that as the learning process that generates higher quality, and lower-cost goods and services has become ever more collective, cumulative and hence complex, strategic investments in organizations that can engage in collective and cumulative learning have become ever more critical to attaining and sustaining competitive advantage (Lazonick, 1993; Lazonick and O'Sullivan, 1995; O'Sullivan, 1996). Market relations provide enterprises with access to productive resources with existing productive capabilities but do not provide the social conditions for the collective and cumulative – or organizational – learning that develops new productive capabilities. The investments in organization required to develop

[5]

productive capabilities depend on the technology concerned and its stage of advance. These investments in organization are also costly. Hence the quality and quantity of investments in organization must be strategic in terms of the potential for the business enterprise to develop and utilize its productive resources (Lazonick, 1991, ch. 3; O'Sullivan, 1996).

In my remarks today I shall summarize how the experiences of the British and American corporate systems over the course of this century support the contention that an organization-oriented model is progressively surpassing a market-oriented model as the social basis for the sustained competitive advantage of enterprises, industries and nations. First, I shall explain how an organization-oriented corporate system contributed to the rise of the United States to economic leadership by the middle decades of this century. I shall then argue that the movement of the US corporate system to a more market-oriented model over the past few decades – a movement that is in part a response to the more highly organized character of Japanese competition – is subverting American prospects for sustained economic prosperity in the decades to come. Then I shall outline how the failure of British industrial enterprises to move towards a much more organization-oriented corporate system was part and parcel of Britain's long-term decline from a position of international economic leadership at the beginning of this century to its current status as a second-rate, even if by global standards still relatively affluent, national economy.

In making the argument about the role of organization-oriented corporate systems in generating competitive advantage and sustained economic growth, I shall focus on the two key social relations that make a corporate system distinctive. One relation, as indicated in *British Factory – Japanese Factory* (Dore, 1990), is the employment of labour. When a business enterprise wants to develop the productive capabilities of labour, the enterprise must not only invest in enhancing and transforming

[6]

the skills of particular people but also create incentives for those people to continue to supply these skills to the company rather than sell them on the market. Such social relations – which represent what we call 'organizational integration' – transform labour from a marketed commodity into a corporate asset (see Lazonick and West, 1995; Lazonick and O'Sullivan, 1996a). The other key social relation is access to finance. When a business enterprise wants to develop its products and processes to generate higher-quality, lower-cost goods and services, it requires ongoing access to financial resources both to sustain the development process and to permit the resources that it has developed to be utilized sufficiently to generate returns that provide the financial liquidity that allows the enterprise to survive. To achieve this ongoing access to finance, the enterprise must exercise organizational control as opposed to market control over its revenues. We call the social relation that secures organizational control over money 'financial commitment' (see Lazonick and O'Sullivan, 1996b; 1996c). Outlining the roles of organizations and markets in the structure and performance of the American and British corporate systems, I shall focus on the ways in which organizational integration and financial commitment have been achieved or undermined.

The American Corporate System

In the late nineteenth and early twentieth centuries a managerial revolution swept American industry. The characteristic features of the managerial revolution were the creation of teams of salaried personnel to plan and co-ordinate the production and distribution of goods and services as well as the separation of legal ownership of corporate assets from control over the allocation of corporate resources and revenues. The fundamental reasons for this organizational transformation were the growing complexity of technology and the increasing scale and scope of market opportunities.

In particular, technological advances in metalworking, chemistry and electronics, themselves often the result of organizational innovation, created possibilities for new technological advances and new technological uses which required new organizational transformations for their development and utilization. The development and utilization of these new technologies required high fixed-cost investments in human and physical assets to acquire inputs, transform them into competitive (high-quality, low-cost) products and distribute these outputs to users. The high fixed costs that resulted from these strategic investments in new technology created pressures to capture new markets to achieve economies of scale and scope.

From this dynamic perspective it should be apparent that technological advances and market opportunities were not independent of the business organizations that were set up to gain privileged access to them. Technological advances and market opportunities were themselves outcomes of prior organizational change, often generated by the business organization through investments in research and development facilities and in marketing capabilities. Especially in industries in which technological innovation and access to mass markets required huge developmental investments, the most successful companies were those which recruited and developed teams of technical specialists and administrators to develop and utilize productive resources in ways that vastly expanded the scale and scope of the goods and services that an enterprise could produce and sell. Increasingly recruited from institutions of higher education, these personnel received in-house training not only within particular technical specialties, germane to the enterprise, but also through rotation or cross-training across technical specialties to permit the integration of specialist activities. Over the course of their careers the most able and willing of these technical specialists were promoted to positions of greater managerial responsibility and authority. These enterprises gained dominant shares of the markets in which they competed, and shaped the development of the national economies in which they emerged.

What ushered in a managerial revolution in the United States was the building of transcontinental railroads in the last decades of the nineteenth century. The first large-scale business enterprises to build managerial organizations, the railroads both enabled the peopling of vast new lands with farmers and artisans and provided the critical communications infrastructure for mass-production enterprises which built managerial organizations to service the demands of these farmers and artisans for capital and consumption goods on a national scale (Chandler, 1977).

Until the last decade of the nineteenth century a formal system of higher education was relatively unimportant for the development and utilization of technology, in part because American industry was only beginning to make the transition from the machine-based first industrial revolution, in which shop-floor experience remained important, to the science-based second industrial revolution, in which systematic formal education was a virtual necessity. From the late nineteenth century, however, the system of higher education became central to supplying technical and managerial personnel to the burgeoning bureaucracies of America's industrial corporations.

Industrial enterprises recruited managerial personnel from the system of higher education and then, through in-house training and on-the-job experience, developed the productive capabilities of these employees and promoted the best of them to middle-level and upper-level managerial positions. That there was room at the top for such career managers had been ensured by the separation of ownership from control (Lazonick, 1986).

Until the great merger movement in that late 1890s and the

early 1900s, the integration of asset ownership and managerial control characterized US industrial enterprises (Chandler, 1990, ch. 3). Before the 1890s a liquid market for the securities of industrial companies did not exist in the United States (Navin and Sears, 1955). Owner–entrepreneurs had to rely on their reputations and connections to raise private capital. They used their own capital as well as that of friends, family and former business associates to launch new ventures, and then relied on retained earnings to transform the enterprises into going concerns. Equity investors had to be prepared to lose their stakes without any possibility of exit via the stock market.

The owner controlled enterprise which had made financial commitments to not only plant and equipment but also the building of integrated managerial organizations were the ones that came to dominate their industries (Chandler, 1977, parts III and IV). It was these types of enterprises with integrated managerial structures that were best positioned to participate in and benefit from the turn-of-the-century merger movement.

With J. P. Morgan taking the lead, Wall Street financed the mergers by selling to the wealth-holding public the ownership stakes of capital-intensive, high-technology companies with integrated managerial structures. The purpose of a public offering of stock was not to fund capital investment in the company but to transfer equity ownership from direct investors to portfolio investors and enable the original owner–entrepreneurs to retire from the industrial scene. With ownership fragmented among hundreds of thousands of shareholders, the new strategic decision makers were professional managers with the power to retain earnings and allocate corporate revenues to innovative investments which built on the organizational and technological capabilities that their enterprises already possessed.

Retained earnings, sometimes leveraged with money raised through long-term bond issues, financed not only state-of-the-art plant and equipment for manufacturing but also the world's most up-to-date research laboratories and far-flung marketing facilities, all of which required investments in the organizational capability to plan and co-ordinate a complex division of labour. The major holders of corporate bonds were the banks and insurance companies which were the prime repositories for household savings (Lazonick, 1992a, pp. 453–4). In a regulated financial environment (which persisted until the 1970s), holders of bank deposits and insurance policies got low but stable returns on their savings while the dominant industrial corporations, with their investment grade ratings from Wall Street, could leverage retained earnings with relatively low-cost debt to finance industrial innovation and expansion.

Until the rise of the institutional investor from the 1960s the holders of common stock were primarily individuals and households. In the early 1950s, for example, financial institutions held about 70 per cent of the corporate bonds outstanding in the United States, but less than 2 per cent of the common stocks (Lazonick, 1992a, pp. 453–4). In the era of US industrial dominance, the markets for bonds and stocks were segmented, with the powerful bondholders largely indifferent to stock yields and the fragmented shareholders unable to influence corporate payout policies. In the allocation of corporate revenues, what Mary O'Sullivan and I call 'organizational control' prevailed (Lazonick and O'Sullivan, 1996b; O'Sullivan, 1996).

With organizationally integrated managerial structures in place and organizational control over corporate revenues providing financial commitment for innovative investment strategies, by the 1920s a number of corporations had consolidated their dominance of their industries. The phenomenal productivity growth that US manufacturing experienced in the 1920s could not have been achieved, however, without managerial success in gaining control over work organization on the shop floor. In the previous decades the managers of the major

[11]

industrial corporations had waged an offensive against the institutions of craft control that had been inherited from the nineteenth century but which, with organizational and technological change, had become inimical to US mass-production methods. To eliminate craft control American managers became obsessed with taking skills off the shop floor and vesting all skill formation in managerial personnel. Meanwhile, in response to this segmented system of skill formation, the evolution of a highly stratified educational system that effectively separated out future managers from future workers even before they entered the workplace left a deep social gulf between managers and workers within US industrial enterprises (Lazonick, 1990, ch. 7–10). Nevertheless, by the 1920s craft control had been defeated, and, by paying shop-floor workers good wages and promising them employment security, the dominant enterprises gained their co-operation in securing high levels of utilization of the high-throughput mass-production technologies that had been put in place.

The Great Depression, however, nullified these efforts at progressive shop-floor management, and deepened dramatically the social separation of management from the shop-floor labour force. During the 1930s the major industrial enterprises kept their managerial organizations intact, and continued to make developmental investments that kept them in the forefront of industrial innovation (Chandler, 1985, pp. 353–61; Mowery, 1986, pp. 191–2; Bernstein, 1987, ch. 4). But, with demand depressed, these same industrial corporations undertook massive layoffs of shop-floor workers. In response, the US labour movement reorganized, but this time on an industrial rather than a craft basis, and used the crisis of the 1930s to wring from the state a measure of economic security for workers that private enterprise had shown itself incapable of providing. When, in the renewed prosperity of the 1940s, dominant mass producers once again sought to gain the co-operation of workers by offering them high wages and prospects of secure employment, they had to deal with powerful mass-production unions. These unions did not challenge the principle of management's right to plan and co-ordinate the shop-floor division of labour (see Lazonick, 1990, ch. 9). In practice, however, the quid pro quo for union co-operation was that seniority be a prime criterion for promotion along well-defined lines and ever more elaborate job structures, thus giving older workers best access to a hierarchical succession of jobs paying gradually rising hourly wage rates. In return, union leadership sought to ensure orderly collective bargaining, including the suppression of unauthorized work stoppages.

Despite the relative absence of skill formation on the shop floor in American industry, the United States emerged as the world's industrial leader in the immediate post-war decades because of its by then unparalleled systems for developing new technologies, especially in the science-based industries. These systems integrated the work of corporate research facilities with those of the government and universities (Kash, 1989). By the late 1950s the intricate linkages that had developed among the government, major corporations and institutions of higher education became known as the 'military–industrial complex'. But even in industries such as automobiles and consumer electronics which relied heavily on the efforts of shop-floor labour, continuous innovation in high-throughput technologies continued to displace the need for skilled shop-floor workers, while union–management co-operation in the co-ordination of shop-floor relations permitted high enough levels of productivity to sustain competitive advantage.

From the 1960s the basic economic conditions that influenced the investment strategies of US industrial corporations began to change in two fundamental ways, one having to do with foreign competition and the other having to do with US financial institutions. Powerful foreign competitors, especially the Japanese, arose to challenge many American companies in the very markets – for example, consumer electronics, mass-produced automobiles, steel – in which they had been world leaders. The structures of co-operative labour–management relations which prevailed in the US era of economic dominance proved problematic when, especially emanating from Japan, more powerful modes of developing and utilizing technology came on the scene. For US corporations to make innovative investments to respond to these competitive challenges, financial commitment became all the more important. Yet, also from the 1960s, the transfer of shareholding from individual investors to institutional investors began to weaken financial commitment as organizational control over the financial resources of US enterprises gave way to market control (Lazonick and O'Sullivan, 1996c).

Compared with institutional investors, individual investors have much less incentive and ability to rearrange their portfolios of securities in search of higher yields. Individuals possess vastly less information about factors affecting stock prices and much higher transaction costs per traded share than institutions. Leading the search for higher yields were the mutual funds that from the 1950s sought to capitalize on the prolonged boom in stock prices. During the 1950s common stocks accounted for 85 per cent of the assets of mutual funds, as compared with about 30 per cent of the assets of pension funds and only 3–4 per cent of the assets of life insurance companies (Lazonick, 1992a, pp. 474–5). Through rapid trading of large blocks of stock and the locking in of capital gains in advance of expected stock declines, mutual fund managers sought to generate higher returns than could be secured from more stable portfolios. The success of the mutual funds in generating higher yields, combined with permissive government deregulation, led pension fund managers to increase their holdings of common stock. In 1955 pension funds owned 2 per cent and households 91 per cent of all equities

[14]

outstanding in the United States; by 1990 the pension fund share had risen to 28 per cent and the household share had fallen to 47 per cent (Lazonick, 1992a, p. 474; Charkham, 1994, p. 204). Insurance companies also gradually increased their holdings of common stocks.

As a result, shareholding ceased to be fragmented in the United States, as households in effect turned to the power of concentrated portfolio management to maximize the returns on their wealth. Mutual funds compete for household savings by showing high returns on a regular basis, and will churn their portfolios in an effort to do so. Pension funds and insurance companies can generally take a longer-run perspective on returns than the mutual funds. Nevertheless, even the portfolio managers of the future-oriented financial institutions are loath to pass up the assured higher returns that, in a speculative financial era, can be made by taking quick capital gains or receiving high levels of dividends.

From the 1960s Wall Street became increasingly devoted to trading in securities, whether stocks or bonds, in preference to its traditional investment-banking function of initial public offerings and long-term corporate bond issues. Indeed, the trading activities of Wall Street combined with institutional investors' quest for higher yields resulted in the integration of the stock and bond markets. High yields achieved through trading in stocks created pressure for bond trading to return similar (risk-adjusted) yields, and high yields in these secondary securities markets put upward pressure on the rates of new bond issues. The rise of the junk-bond market from the mid 1970s in turn put pressure on the stock market to generate higher short-term returns, which in turn placed demands on companies to increase dividends. The high yields secured by portfolio investors then made it impossible for commercial banks, mutual banks, and savings and loan companies to attract deposits on the basis of the old rules of the financial game. Financial deregulation in the late 1970s enabled these financial intermediaries to join the search for higher short-term yields. By the early 1980s, all of these changes in the structure of US financial markets created opportune conditions for the junk-bond financed corporate raider. The market for corporate control had been unleashed.

Changes in the relation between ownership and management during the 1950s, 1960s and 1970s increased the incentive and the ability of the top managers of major US industrial corporations to ally with the forces that sought financial liquidity rather than financial commitment. From the early 1950s, through the use of stock-options, the total remuneration of top managers became increasingly dependent on stock-based rewards. In the late 1940s a sample consisting of the top five executives of 50 Fortune 500 companies derived less than 3 per cent of their after-tax compensation from stock-based awards; a decade later this figure was over 30 per cent (Lewellen, 1968, pp. 172–3; Lewellen, 1971, p. 50). This access of top managers to substantial amounts of ownership income weakened their incentives to choose innovative investment strategies. Like shareholders in general, these new owner-managers benefited handsomely from financial institutions and instruments that sought to generate revenues on the basis of past accumulation while neglecting investment for the future. By boosting short-term profits, top managers saw the market value of their shares rise, which in turn justified increasing dividends to maintain yields and which in turn reduced the retained earnings available for investment in organization and technology.

Through the integration of ownership and control at the top of the corporate hierarchy, top managers in effect set themselves apart from the rest of the organizational structure. This separation became amply manifest during the 1980s in an explosion of top-management pay. While the real average after-tax earnings of American wage and salary earners fell by 13 per cent during the 1970s and 1980s, the real average after-tax compensation of CEOs of major American corporations increased by 400 per cent. In 1981 the average compensation of the 25 highest-paid executives of US non-financial enterprises was $2.46 million; by 1988 this figure was almost five times higher at $12.22 million (Phillips, 1990, p. 179).

The value-extracting capabilities of American top executives became particularly evident when their compensation was compared with that of their counterparts abroad. In 1990 the salary and bonus compensation of CEOs of the 30 largest US corporations was on average $3.1 million. For British CEOs (who had also increased their power to extract value from earlier decades) the comparable figure was $1.1 million; for French and German CEOs, $0.8 million; and for Japanese CEOs $0.5 million (*New York Times*, 1992). The availability of stock options to American top managers, but not to Japanese top managers, made the international gap in CEO compensation all the more striking – especially when, as was increasingly the case, the enterprises that Japanese managers directed were outcompeting the enterprises over which the American managers presided.

In the 1990s many American corporations are striving to compete by downsizing, often under the euphemism of 're-engineering'. These corporations are often in dire need of organizational and technological change. By terminating thousands of employees, an established company can restore profitability and boost its stock price, but without necessarily making the new investments in products, processes and people that are essential for sustained competitive success. Indeed, the higher profits and stock prices provide a justification for higher dividends that maintain stock yields. The proportion of after-tax corporate profits of US non-financial corporations distributed as dividends rose from about 45 per cent in the 1960s and 1970s to 60 per cent in the 1980s and to well over 60 per cent in the early 1990s (*Economic Report of the President*, 1995, p. 379). While yields on portfolio investments have remained high, financial commitment for industrial innovation continues to erode. The problem of financial commitment is not just a dispersion of mobilized capital from productive enterprises but, more fundamentally, an alignment of top managers, as strategic decision makers, with the forces for value extraction rather than value creation (see Lazonick, 1994b).

The British Corporate System

In the 1990s the financially driven character of the American corporate system bears a marked resemblance to the British corporate system. In comparative historical perspective, however, what is unique about Britain is the nation's failure to mount a managerial revolution during this century (Elbaum and Lazonick, 1986; Lazonick, 1986; Chandler, 1990, part III). Britain's twentieth-century experience is in many ways a legacy of the social foundations of its rise to international economic leadership in the nineteenth century. The nation's rise to industrial power depended on industry structures that were regionally concentrated, vertically specialized and horizontally fragmented into small-scale proprietary firms. These enterprises relied on skilled workers rather than managerial personnel to plan and co-ordinate work on the shop floor. The lack of managerial organization in turn reinforced the tendency for industrial structures to be fragmented and specialized. Limited in their managerial capabilities, proprietary firms tended to confine themselves to single-plant operations, thus facilitating the entry of new firms into vertical specialties and increasing the extent of horizontal as well as vertical fragmentation of industrial sectors.

The prime source of the development of productive capabilities in the industrial districts of nineteenth-century Britain was the skilled labour required to operate technologies that, even when mechanized, were highly imperfect. With the rise of managerial capitalism abroad in the twentieth century, the persistence of craft-based and market co-ordinated industrial structures that had carried the British economy to international dominance in the nineteenth century constituted impediments to the development and utilization of advanced technology. Whereas the success of the managerial revolution in the United States resulted in a transformation of organization and technology that eliminated craft control, a characteristic feature of British industry in the twentieth century was the persistence of craft control (Lazonick, 1900, ch. 6).

In the staple industries – iron and steel, shipbuilding, mechanical engineering and textiles – that had brought Britain to economic supremacy, more organizational capability resided in craft control on the shop floor than in the underdeveloped managerial structures (see Lazonick, 1990, ch. 6). Insofar as British craft workers continued to co-operate with their employers in the twentieth century, it was in squeezing as much productivity as possible out of the *existing* technologies, often by failing to maintain the quality of the product and driving their shop-floor assistants as well as themselves to supply more effort. As it became necessary in order to retain their jobs, they also accepted lower wages. Immobile because of their highly specialized skills, both workers and employers had the incentives to ensure the survival of the firms through which they gained their livelihoods. Many British firms in the staple industries were able to survive for decades by living off the plant, equipment, infrastructures and skills accumulated in the era of British industrial leadership (Elbaum and Lazonick, 1986).

In some industries (mechanical engineering in particular) employers tried to use their collective power to break craft control over the organization of work and the determination of remuneration. Even when employers rolled back prior union

[19]

gains, however, craft control was not eliminated, in large part because proprietary capitalists, lacking managerial organizations, had no organizational alternatives with which to replace craft control. What is more, even in a new machine-based industry such as automobile manufacture, in which the craft unions were not already ensconced, shop-floor control on the craft model became dominant in the first decades of the twentieth century as the automobile manufacturers tended to rely on craft workers to plan and co-ordinate the flow of work on the shop floor (Lazonick, 1990, ch. 6).

Reliance on shop-floor workers to perform what we now consider to be managerial functions continued during the interwar period, even in firms such as Austin and Morris that were becoming dominant mass producers for the British market (Lewchuk, 1987). In the 1940s and 1950s, under conditions of tight labour markets combined with the limited opportunities for firms that relied on labour-intensive technologies to generate new sources of productivity, these workers used the shop-floor organizational responsibilities that had been delegated to them as the foundations on which to build specialized craft unions. The result was that by the 1960s one could find scores of separate craft agreements in place at any point in time in any one automobile plant, with the resultant fragmentation of employer–employee relations placing severe constraints on managerial co-ordination of the specialized division of labour within the plant.

Yet the British automobile industry remained viable in global competition until the 1960s because of its low fixed costs (including the almost complete neglect of research and development) as well as the acceptance of relatively low returns by workers, managers and owners. The 1960s and 1970s revealed, however, that like the staple industries of the nineteenth century, the British automobile industry had reached the technical and social limits of the utilization of its resources. Facing the continued development of continental producers as well as the rise of the Japanese automobile manufacturers, the economic viability of the British industry could no longer be sustained.

The development of organizational capability was somewhat different in the science-based industries of the second industrial revolution – chemicals, rubber, electrical equipment and appliances – in which it was impossible to enter into competition on the basis of technological capabilities inherited from the past. Largely through the efforts of dedicated and aggressive entrepreneurs (typically, although not always, owners as well as managers) who either developed new technologies or controlled foreign patents, a number of British firms such as Lever Brothers, Pilkington Brothers, Dunlop, Courtaulds, Crosfield's, Nobel's, and Brunner, Mond, were able to become strong global competitors in the late nineteenth and early twentieth centuries (for business histories, see Wilson, 1984; Barker, 1977; Jones, 1984; Coleman, 1969; Musson, 1965; Reader, 1975).

Nevertheless, after the turn of the century the largest British firms were not only much smaller than the largest US companies, but also much more under the control of family ownership. Unlike the United States where, from the turn of the century, ownership was separated from control, in Britain the social-class structure in combination with the educational system and the financial system abetted the continued integration of ownership and control.

British industrialists of the late nineteenth century were generally middle class, with their home bases in the industrial districts of the Midlands and the North. Among those engaged in business, large accumulations of wealth and substantial political power were in the hands, not of these industrialists, but of financiers based in the City of London. Using upper-class educational institutions as means of entry and marriages as instruments of merger, wealthy financiers joined with the old landowning elite (many of them grown recently wealthy through rising land values) to form a new aristocracy. The wealth of this

[21]

restructured upper class was not, as was increasingly the case in the United States and Germany, based on the application of science to industry and the resultant profits from technological innovation. Rather, their wealth was based on financial activities, for which social connections and acquired reputations were the keys to success.

For individuals, the accumulation of such 'social assets' began at elite educational institutions – Oxford and Cambridge as well as public schools such as Eton and Harrow. Lacking industrial roots, the aristocracy who controlled these elite institutions during the era of the second industrial revolution had no need for an educational system that developed technologists. They valued the study of science as a branch of sophisticated knowledge, but had no interest in its application to industry. Nor did successful industrialists who accumulated fortunes sufficient to join Britain's upper class effectively challenge the anti-industry bias of Britain's elite educational system. Of middle-class, or even working-class, backgrounds, Britain's most successful industrialists sought to elevate their social standing by distancing themselves from the technological roots of their prior advance. They typically located their head offices in London, far from industrial production. They sent their sons to be educated at the public schools and, if possible, at Oxbridge, to network with an aristocracy that was anti-technology. Hence these industrialists, and particularly the most successful among them, did not see it as in their interests to transform the nation's premier educational institutions into servants of industry. Their goal was rather to partake of aristocratic culture to serve their aspirations for upward mobility, which meant accepting the anti-technology bias of that culture. As the historian Donald Coleman (1973) has put it in a well-known essay, successful industrialists sought to become 'gentlemen' rather than 'players'.

As successful British industrialists sought to move up the social hierarchy, control over established industrial enterprises remained the foundations of their material wealth and the most assured means of passing wealth on to their children. They brought their sons and sons-in-law in to manage their businesses, thus perpetuating the integration of family ownership and control. The larger owner-controlled firms that, because of enterprise expansion or a dearth of qualified family members, had to recruit top managers from outside the family, gave highest preference to young men with a classical Oxbridge education. As a result, the most influential British industrialists put little pressure on the elite schools and universities to educate the future captains of industry in matters concerning business organization and industrial technology (see Lazonick, 1986; 1991, ch. 1; 1994a).

By virtue of such educational backgrounds and social aspirations, increasingly those in control of British industrial enterprises in the first half of the twentieth century were not themselves well equipped or well positioned to lead their companies in the pursuit of technological innovation. Within the enterprise, top managers of the most successful enterprises of the second industrial revolution set themselves apart as an elite social class, thus creating an organizational barrier between themselves as strategic decision makers and the technical specialists who were expected to implement enterprise strategies. Increasingly after the turn of the century, many of the technical specialists employed by science-based enterprises came from the newly established provincial universities that did try to cater to the educational needs of technologists. The second-class status of the graduates of the provincial universities was confirmed, however, when they took up employment in major British industrial enterprises. Because of the way the top managers of the personally managed enterprises were recruited, these technical specialists could not view their initial employment in even the larger enterprises as a first step up a managerial hierarchy that might ultimately lead to positions of strategic control. As a result of these barriers to social mobility within the enterprise, technical specialists were less committed than they might otherwise have been to furthering enterprise goals and more likely to view interfirm mobility as the main route to career progress. Such prospects of employee exit in turn reduced the incentive for these enterprises to invest in the productive capabilities of these technical specialists. Even in the cases of trained scientists and engineers, therefore, leading British enterprises relied more on market co-ordination than management co-ordination in their employment of labour (see Dore, 1990). In industries in which the development and utilization of technology depended on the development and utilization of highly specialized technical skills, enterprises which relied on market co-ordinated employment relations could find themselves at a decided disadvantage in global competition.

A weakness of organizational integration within the managerial hierarchies of British industrial enterprises was matched by a weakness of financial commitment to developmental investments. In Britain, as in the other advanced economies, retained earnings formed the financial basis of enterprise growth for going concerns. When, from the late nineteenth century, existing family-owned enterprises needed to supplement retained earnings to invest in plant and equipment, they often issued fixed interest securities to the public. The favoured financial instrument was the non-voting preferred share, a security which paid a higher return than a debenture (or bond) but which avoided both any loss of proprietary control and any risk of being forced into bankruptcy (Jefferys, 1977, ch. 5).

Another source of finance, both short-term and long-term, was the bank overdraft. The ostensible purpose of overdraft privileges was to enable a firm to smooth out its cash flow. In practice, however, many firms used bank overdrafts for fixed-capital investment. As long as these firms achieved high levels of capacity utilization of these investments, this mode of financing did not cause problems. In periods such as the 1920s, however, when, after the speculative recapitalization of firms in the post-war boom, whole industrial sectors such as steel and textiles experienced prolonged recession, many bank overdrafts became bad loans. To pay these debts, limited liability companies had to call in their unpaid share capital, which led to large withdrawals of shareholders' deposit accounts in local banks, thus putting further pressure on these banks to make good on their loan portfolios (Tolliday, 1986; Bamberg, 1988).

By the end of the 1920s the banks took the lead in industry-wide rationalizations that compelled debt-ridden firms to combine through amalgamation into larger enterprises under centralized managerial control. To effect these amalgamations owners of the constituent firms, as well as debtors, were issued ordinary shares in the new company, thus weakening but not severing the integration of ownership and control. The old owners still retained substantial decision-making authority in the amalgamated structure because of the intimate knowledge they had of the operations of their particular businesses and the absence of general management capabilities in British industry (see Hannah, 1983, ch. 3). Yet, because the banks could ultimately force a firm to join the amalgamation or got out of business, these bank-dictated amalgamations went much further in separating ownership from control than most other industrial combinations in Britain during the first half of the century. In virtually all industries, including newer ones such as electrical engineering and chemicals, proprietary firms in the same industry amalgamated for the purpose of controlling product prices, the amalgamation being effected by issuing stock in the new company. Such merger activity was particularly marked in the periods 1919–20 and 1927–9 (Hannah, 1983, p. 93). Within the amalgamated structure, however, the constituent businesses maintained their proprietary independence, thus impeding the use of the amalgamation to rationalize product lines and engage

[25]

in co-operative activities such as research and marketing (Chandler, 1980; Hannah, 1983, ch. 7).

Over time, as the shareholders in these amalgamations sold their stakes on the market, share ownership became divorced from managerial control, but without leaving in place integrated managerial organizations to plan and co-ordinate innovative investment strategies. By the 1940s and 1950s even firms that had successfully remained proprietary took advantage of a growing demand by portfolio investors for corporate equities and liquidated their holdings by issuing ordinary (that is, common) shares to the public (Thomas, 1978, ch. 6). By the early 1950s the preferred shares which had been so popular when ownership had remained integrated with control had fallen into disuse (Thomas, 1978, p. 159). Given the organizational weaknesses of these public companies for developing and utilizing technology, public shareholders had a greater incentive to exercise market control in Britain compared with their counterparts in the United States. A realistic assessment of the long-run potential of these companies encouraged shareholders to try to reap the returns of the past rather than reinvest for the future. Beginning in the 1950s, moreover, British institutional investors began to wield their power to extract high returns from their industrial portfolios, even somewhat ahead of the rise of collective shareholding in the United States. Already in the late 1950s the British economy experienced a hostile takeover movement which made the managers of industrial enterprises reluctant to retain large reserves of liquid assets that could underwrite innovative investments (Thomas, 1978, p. 22; Charkham, 1994, p. 303ff).

Coming into the era of unmitigated financial deregulation of the 1980s, financial commitment in Britain was already weak by international comparison. During the 1980s international competition and capital movements, combined with the quest for higher yields on portfolio investments, created pressures to

[26]

weaken organizational control in all the advanced economies. In Britain, even more than in the United States, the deregulated financial environment of the 1980s advanced the power of market control and eroded financial commitment. Dividends and stock prices soared, as did the salaries of top managers of industrial enterprises who co-operated with the forces of market control (see Charkham, 1994, ch. 6). In 1987 the market capitalization of quoted companies was 86 per cent of the value of GDP in Britain but only 16 per cent in Germany (Charkham, 1994, p. 301). By the 1980s and early 1990s payout ratios of British non-financial corporations persistently exceeded the high payout ratios of American companies by between 5 per cent and 20 per cent (*Economist*, 1994, p. 109). As Charkham (1994, p. 312) has put it in his recent survey of corporate governance in Japan, Germany, France, United States, and Britain:

> In some respects UK industry is at a continuing competitive disadvantage against countries in which market pressures are not so severe. Much of this is a paraphrase of the US situation, but just as much a matter of concern to the one country as the other. The UK is vulnerable against those who play with different rules, in that their networked systems of accountability work effectively without management having to live in fear of the market: these tend to have more latitude for investments which take longer to pay off.

And as, in 1992, Gottfried Bruder, Commerzbank's general manager in London, summed up the rhetoric and reality of market control in Britain:

> The proponents of a stock exchange dominated culture, who with stars in their eyes point to the liquid London Stock Exchange and its vastly larger turnover than that of its continental rivals, normally answer with the most platitudinal clichés when one asks them who the beneficiaries of these

[27]

impressive turnovers are. Whatever their answer is, it is certainly not British industry. (Quoted in Charkham, 1994, p. 56.)

The Anglo-Saxon System in the Global Economy

Let me conclude my comparison of the American and British corporate systems with some observations concerning the implications of their similarities and differences for understanding the future of corporate systems in the global economy. Currently, both systems show a marked propensity, which manifests their market orientation, to live off the past rather than invest for the future – to extract value rather than create value (see Lazonick, 1994b). Compared with organization-oriented corporate systems which develop the productive resources that they then utilize, market-oriented corporate systems, such as those that currently prevail in the United States and Britain, tend to focus on the utilization of resources that were developed in the past.

But the historical comparison of the evolution of the American and British corporate systems shows that this similarity in market orientation has not always been the case. The organization orientation of the American system, embodied in the century-old managerial revolution, enabled the United States to develop and utilize productive resources in a way that was beyond the capability of the much more market-oriented British system. A correct understanding of the American experience demonstrates that the success of organization-oriented corporate systems in global competition is not something that was invented by the Japanese. The problem for the United States today is that it is failing to extend and transform the organizational capabilities that made it successful in the past as it is being challenged by global competitors who have put in place even

[28]

more powerful organization-oriented systems (see Lazonick and Mass, 1995; Lazonick and O'Sullivan, 1995). The problem for Britain today is that, among the advanced economies, it made the least progress in the twentieth century in building the organizational capabilities required for sustained competitive advantage (see Lazonick, 1992b).

The most important productive resources that organization-oriented corporate systems develop are human resources, because it is people, with their knowledge, learning and skills, who develop physical resources. The need for organization derives from the power of collective and cumulative character of the learning required to develop and utilize complex technology. By investing in the productive capabilities of people as members of learning organizations, a corporate system can transform labour from a commodity marketed by individuals into an asset that works collectively.

A recognition of the centrality of organizational learning to sustained economic development raises critical questions about how we evaluate the performance of corporate systems and, ultimately, about how we govern them (see O'Sullivan, 1996). In a world that is increasingly driven by financial markets that, by laying claim to corporate assets, live off the past, investment for the future must be guided by organization-oriented rather than market-oriented measures of performance – something that 'modern' accounting systems do not currently provide. Specifically, we need to measure investments in the productive capabilities of people and account for these investments in human capabilities as part of the corporate asset base. From this organization-oriented perspective, it follows that the higher earnings that people may receive by developing and utilizing their productive capabilities should be evaluated as returns on these corporate assets, and hence as a measure of the success of corporate investments. Instead, 'modern' accounting systems, reflecting their market orientation, regard investments in people as well as the returns from these investments which people receive as current expenses that adversely affect current profits. In an era which favours downsizing to investing, market-oriented accounting systems measure economic failure as economic success, and economic success as economic failure.

Finally, I should point out the ideology that supports the market orientation of the Anglo-Saxon corporate system is not simply the creation of greedy corporate executives, financial manipulators and money managers – although they have acquired a big stake in the ideology. As I have argued in detail elsewhere (Lazonick, 1991), the theoretical foundations for the superiority of the market-oriented economy are found in the theory of the market economy, better known as neo-classical economics, which virtually all students of economics in the advanced economies are not only taught but are also taught to believe as irrefutable gospel. We need to replace this a-historical ideology with a theory that can comprehend the organizational foundations of economic development and competitive advantage in comparative and historical perspective. The building of such a relevant theory need not be just an academic exercise – the wealth of nations, and the livelihoods of millions of people in those nations, may depend on it.

References

Abbeglen, J. C. (1958): *The Japanese Factory*, Mission Hills, CA: Glencoe, New York, NY: Free Press.

Amsden, A. (1989): *Asia's Next Giant: South Korea and Late Industriali-zation*. Oxford: Oxford University Press.

Bamberg, J. H. (1988): The rationalization of the British cotton industry in the interwar years. *Textile History*, no. 19, p. 1.

Barker, T. C. (1977): *The Glassmakers: Pilkington: The Rise of an International Company, 1826–1976*. London: Weidenfeld & Nicolson.

Bernstein, M. (1987): *The Great Depression: Delayed Recovery and Economic Change in America, 1929–1939*. Cambridge: Cambridge University Press.

Chandler, Jr. A. D. (1977): *The Visible Hand: The Managerial Revolution in American Business*. Cambridge, MA: Harvard University Press.

—— (1980): The growth of the transnational industrial firm in the United States and the United Kingdom: a comparative analysis. *Economic History Review*, 2nd series, 33 (August).

—— (1985): From industrial laboratories to departments of research and development. In K. B. Clark, R. H. Hayes and C. Lorenz (eds), *The Uneasy Alliance: Managing the Productivity–Technology Dilemma*. Boston, MA: Harvard Business School Press.

—— (1990): *Scale and Scope: The Dynamics of Industrial Capitalism*. Cambridge, MA: Harvard University Press.

Charkham, J. (1994): *Keeping Good Company: A Study of Corporate Governance in Five Countries*. Oxford: Clarendon Press.

Coleman, D. C. (1969): *Courtaulds: An Economic and Social History*, vol. 1. Oxford: Clarendon Press.

—— (1973): Gentlemen and players. *Economic History Review*, 2nd series, 26.

Dore, R. (1973): *British Factory–Japanese Factory: The Origins of National Diversity in Industrial Relations*. Berkeley, CA: University of California Press.

—— (1990): *British Factory–Japanese Factory: The Origins of National Diversity in Industrial Relations*, 2nd edn. Berkeley, CA: University of California Press.

Economic Report of the President (1995): Washington, DC: United States Government Printing Office.

Economist (1994), 4 June.

Elbaum, B. and W. Lazonick (eds) (1986): *The Decline of the British Economy*. Oxford: Oxford University Press.

Hannah, L. (1983): *The Rise of the Corporate Economy*, 2nd edn. Baltimore, MD: Johns Hopkins University Press.

—— (1986): *Inventing Retirement: The Development of Occupational Pensions in Britain*. Cambridge: Cambridge University Press.

Jefferys, J. B. (1977): *Business Organisation in Great Britain, 1856–1914*. Salem, NH: Arno Press (first pub. 1938).

[31]

Jones, G. (1984): The growth and performance of British multinational firms before 1939: the case of Dunlop. *Economic History Review,* 2nd series, 37 (February).

Jong, H. W. de (1994): European capitalism: between freedom and social justice. Photocopy. Amsterdam: University of Amsterdam.

—— (1995): European capitalism: between freedom and social justice. In *Review of Industrial Organization,* vol. 8, no. 4 (August).

Kash, D. (1989): *Perpetual Innovation: The New World of Competition.* New York, NY: Basic Books.

Lazonick, W. (1986): Strategy, structure, and management development in the United States and Britain. In K. Kobayashi and H. Morikawa (eds). *Development of Managerial Enterprise.* Tokyo: University of Tokyo Press (Reprinted in W. Lazonick (1992): *Organization and Technology in Capitalist Development.* Aldershot: Elgar Publishing.)

—— (1990): *Competitive Advantage on the Shop Floor.* Cambridge, MA: Harvard University Press.

—— (1991): *Business Organization and the Myth of the Market Economy.* Cambridge: Cambridge University Press.

—— (1992a): Controlling the market for corporate control: the historical significance of managerial capitalism. *Industrial and Corporate Change,* no. 1, p. 3.

—— (1992b): *Organization and Technology in Capitalist Development.* Aldershot: Elgar Publishing.

—— (1993): Learning and the dynamics of international competitive advantage. In R. Thomson (ed.), *Learning and Technical Change.* London: Macmillan.

—— (1994a): Social organization and technological leadership. In W. J. Baumol, R. R. Nelson and E. N. Wolff (eds), *Convergence of Productivity: Cross National Studies and Historical Evidence.* Oxford: Oxford University Press.

—— (1994b): Creating and extracting value: corporate investment behavior and American economic performance. In M. A. Bernstein and D. E. Adler (eds), *Understanding American Economic Decline.* Cambridge: Cambridge University Press.

—— and Mass, W. (1995) (eds): *Organizational Capability and Competitive Advantage.* Aldershot: Elgar Publishing.

—— and West, J. (1995): Organizational integration and competitive advantage: explaining strategy and performance in American industry. *Industrial and Corporate Change*, 4, 2.

—— and O'Sullivan, M. (1995): The Governance of innovation for economic development. Research report to Studies on Technology, Innovation, and Economic Policy (STEP) Group (Oslo), August.

—— and O'Sullivan, M. (1996a): Organization, finance, and international competition. *Industrial and Corporate Change*, 5, 1 (forthcoming).

—— and O'Sullivan, M. (1996b): Financial commitment and economic development: the persistence of organizational control. *Financial History Review* (forthcoming).

—— and O'Sullivan, M. (1996c): Financial commitment and economic development: the evolution of market control. *Financial History Review* (forthcoming).

—— and O'Sullivan, M. (1996d): Big business and skill formation in the wealthiest nations: the organizational revolution in the twentieth century. In F. Amatori, A. D. Chandler, Jr. and T. Hikino, *Big Business and the Wealth of Nations*. Cambridge: Cambridge University Press (forthcoming).

Lewchuk, W. (1987): *American Technology and the British Vehicle Industry*. Cambridge: Cambridge University Press.

Lewellen, W. G. (1968): *Executive Compensation in Large Industrial Corporations*. National Bureau of Economic Research.

—— (1971): *The Ownership Income of Management*. National Bureau of Economic Research.

Mowery, D. C. (1986): Industrial research, 1900–1950. In B. Elbaum and W. Lazonick (eds), *The Decline of the British Economy*. Oxford: Oxford University Press.

Musson, A. E. (1965): *Enterprise in Soap and Chemicals*. Manchester: Manchester University Press.

Navin, Th. R. and Sears, M. V. (1955): The rise of a market for industrial securities, 1887–1902. *Business History Review*, 29, June.

New York Times (1992), 20 January.

Oliver, N. and Wilkinson, B. (1992): *The Japanization of British Industry*, 2nd edn. Oxford: Blackwell Publishers Ltd.

O'Sullivan, M.: Business governance and industrial development: who are the principals?, Ph.D. dissertation. Cambridge, MA: Harvard University (forthcoming).

Phillips, K. (1990): *The Politics of Rich and Poor*. London: Random House.

Reader, W. J. (1975): *Imperial Chemical Industries*, vol. I. Oxford: Oxford University Press.

Strange, R. (1993): *Japanese Manufacturing Investment in Europe: Its Impact on the UK Economy*. London: Routledge.

Thomas, W. A. (1978): *The Finance of British Industry, 1918–1976*. Methuen.

Tolliday, S. (1986): Steel and rationalization policies, 1918–1950. In B. Elbaum and W. Lazonick (eds), *The Decline of the British Economy*. Oxford: Oxford University Press.

Wade, R. (1990): *Governing The Market: Economic Theory and the Role of Government in East Asian Industrialization*. Princeton, NJ: Princeton University Press.

Wilson, Ch. (1984): *The History of Unilever*, vol. I. Cambridge: Cambridge University Press.

World Bank (1992): *The East Asian Miracle*.

2

The Asian Form of Capitalism

Ronald Dore

I suppose there are economists who view the economy as dispassionately as, say, a metallurgist views a lump of unknown metal, but most of us find it hard to separate our economics from our value system and our citizenship. We may try to be as dispassionate as the metallurgist, to muster all our powers of objective analysis, but most of us do so in order to find better ways of organizing society, in particular our own society.

So, the comparison of different capitalist systems which we are undertaking here today inevitably has the underlying question, 'which is better?', although we may conceal the evaluation by asking 'which gives the better performance?' as if performance were an objectively measurable parameter. But of course it is not. By 'performance' most people mean a mix of GDP growth rates, share of world markets, plus perhaps some measures which have as much to do with distribution as with growth, like inflation control and employment/unemployment. But the weighting of these different criteria depends on one's individual values.

Take, for instance, the choice of targets which the European Round Table of industrialists – composed of the heads of some 42 of the biggest firms in Europe from Fiat and Olivetti to Unilever, Shell and Philips – proposed, in a document for the Cannes EU summit meeting earlier this year, should be used as benchmarks to measure 'the progress of European competitiveness' ERT (1995). The word 'competitiveness' already privileges one of the aspects of performance, namely share in world markets, which they propose Europe should get back to the 25 per cent mark, reversing the steady decline over the last 12 years. That requires a shift from consumption to investment – an increase in the savings rate from its current 20 per cent European average to 25 per cent, which is target number one. Their third target – the creation of 10 million new jobs by the end of the century – most people would agree with. We only want to know how on earth to do it. Its fifth – achieving a balance of technological payments by earning as much from the sale of intellectual property and knowhow as we pay other countries – may not be so well conceived. Japan, for instance, continues to have deficits in technology payments not because the Japanese do not do a lot of creative R&D, but because Japanese firms have a better system of technological reconnaissance and are more open to learning from the outside world than more complacent Western firms.

Profit versus Value Added

But, to my mind, most controversial of all is their second target; the pre-tax rate of return on capital which they estimate to average 14 per cent in Europe, should be raised. The American level of 19 per cent they think perhaps too much to hope for; but at least Europe should manage 17 per cent by the end of the decade.

Now consider the following argument. Return on capital is a measure of the efficiency with which the owners of capital or their agents use that capital to command the use of all resources, including labour which is treated as an employed resource like any other. To put it crudely, it is a measure not only of how

[36]

cleverly you can use material objects, but also of how efficiently you can screw your workers. It is anything but distribution neutral. Consider the Japanese economy which has much lower rates of return on capital, lower rates of growth in shareholder value, but nevertheless does better on the other criteria of savings, growth rates, share of world markets and employment.[1] A much more distribution-neutral measure of performance, one for which Henk de Jong has been constructing a pioneering database, would be value-added per capital employed.

Underlying the choice between the two measures – profits and value added – is a choice between two concepts of the firm. On the one hand is the concept, taken for granted by the dominant majority of the economics profession, and particularly by all the clever games-theorist analysts of the principal-agent relationship, of the firm as an entity run by agents of the owners of capital solely for the profits of the latter. On the other is the concept of the firm as a group of people engaged in the co-operative and co-ordinated activity of using both the capital they can borrow or get its owners to put at risk with them, together with their own energies and intellectual resources, to create value. In this view, how much value they succeed in creating is the real performance/competitiveness question. How much of the created value then goes to those who supplied the capital and how much goes to those who supplied the energy and intellectual resources is then a second-order question, but one which is of great interest from the point of view of two very pertinent questions. The first is the unresolvable value question: what sort of distribution most accords with social justice? The second is an empirical question: what sort of distribution provides the optimal motivation, on the one hand to the suppliers of capital and on the other to the suppliers of the energy and intellectual resources – optimal in the sense of improving value-creation performance? De Jong's demonstration of the wide differences among European countries in the pattern of distribution of value added as between capital and labour puts that latter, empirical, question squarely on the agenda. It is a pity that, for every one economist interested in taking it up, there are ten searching for an ever-more clever piece of algebra with which to contribute to principal-agent theory.

Globalization and Capital Flows

Nevertheless, the European Round Table set its targets in terms of profits rather than value added. Why? The answer is not quite as simple as the fact that it is a roundtable of industrial managers, not of trade unionists. It has rather to do with the fact that, for what they consider good reasons, they give an answer to that last question about the motivational consequences of the distribution of value added which gives overwhelming priority to the owners of capital. (Or rather to the pension fund and investment trust managers of capital; the owners are increasingly the pension fund members who are, paradoxically, at the same time the producers of the energy and intellectual resources.) We live in a capitalist, not a labourist, world economy. The internationally mobile factor of production – and particularly the trans-Atlantically mobile factor – is capital, not labour. Unless Europe raises its rewards to capital, relative to that of the US, they argue, its savings will increasingly 'go West', across the Atlantic to the United States.

The pattern of British and Dutch investment over the last ten years and its distribution as between Europe and the United States – not so much portfolio investment as the direct investment of retained earnings by business firms – provides some justification for that argument. But why is it then that, in spite of the much lower returns to equity capital in Japan after the end of the late 1980s bubble and the collapse of share values on the stock market, Japanese capital still tends to stay at home, and the Japanese stock market even benefits from a good deal of portfolio investment from abroad? Japanese banks cry out that they are hurting and need government support because of the debt overhang left by the collapse of the asset price bubble, but there is so little evidence of a shortage of credit in Japan that the Government and the Bank of Japan can afford to try to stimulate recovery with a bank rate of 0.5 per cent.

The answer to the question why Japanese capital stays at home probably lies in the exchange rate. Japanese insurance companies have been caught before with a halving of the yen value of their dollar portfolio as a result of dramatic exchange rate shifts. The long-term trend of the yen is still upwards, and for all the higher returns foreign firms may offer, the risk that those higher returns might be drastically reduced by currency shifts serve as a deterrent. It appears that their recent dollar-security buying spree was as much what we used to call a 'Japan Inc. phenomenon' as a self-interested pursuit of profit. They agreed to co-operate in a concerted attempt to strengthen the dollar for the sake of Japanese exporters and hence of the Japanese economy as a whole.

The Two Views of the Firm

One wonders, though, whether there are not other factors involved in the preference of Japanese capital to stay at home. One factor, of course, is that much more of it is invested through loan arrangements negotiated person to person rather than through anonymous equity purchase, and Japanese, for a variety of cultural and linguistic reasons, prefer to deal with other Japanese – the main reason for the famed impenetrability of the Japanese market. But there is also, I suspect, a preference for lending money to firms which are of the Japanese type, rather than to firms which are of what, to use Michel Albert's categories (see Albert 1991; 1993), one might call the Anglo-Saxon type. Just now, I drew a contrast between the concept of the firm as an entity run by agents of the capital-owning principals with the sole objective of maximizing the profits of the latter, and, on the other hand, the concept of the firm as a group of people engaged in the co-operative and co-ordinated activity of using both the capital they can borrow or get its owners to put at risk with them, together with their own energies and intellectual resources, to create value. As the empirically-grounded theorists of Anglo-Saxon type firms, from Penrose to Herbert Simon and Chandler have shown, their actual operation is a good deal removed from the simple profit-maximizing characterization which I have just given, but nevertheless there is enough plausibility in that caricature for principal-agent theory, which treats it as the essential reality, to have become a flourishing branch of economics.

And the Japanese firm – the typical large Japanese firm – is the best living exemplar of the contrasting, what I will call the 'firm as community', paradigm. Let me spell out some of the ways in which the two types of firm are contrasted – in the manner of their financing, their structures, their reaction to business cycles, their patterns of accountability and reward. Arguably, the keystone of the whole structure is the mode of financing. Japanese company law differs remarkably little from Anglo-Saxon company law. The managers are clearly defined as agents of the shareholders. It is the shareholders who legally constitute the 'membership' of the company, not the employees towards which the company has no other obligations beyond those specified by the employment contract, however that contract may be modified by labour law and so on with which the Commercial Code is not concerned. In effect, however, the shareholders' influence is neutralized, partly because, ever since the last war, firms have come to rely more on bank loans than on equity, and partly because most large Japanese firms have the bulk of their shares in the hands of the banks with whom they do their loan business, or with the insurance companies with whom they do their insurance business, or with other industrial and commercial companies with whom they do a lot of their trading. And with these latter, as with their banks, a good deal of their shareholding is on a reciprocal basis; Hitachi owns several million Nissan shares and vice versa.

One major consequence of this – again an evolution from a pre-existing Anglo-Saxon type capitalist system which took place during the war – is that the CEOs and the directors of Japanese firms are predominantly not shareholder representatives but career managers who have in most cases spent the whole of their careers in the firm and have been promoted through exactly the same bureaucratic structures as ensure that in most traditional European civil services those who get to be department heads are the most able of the senior career civil servants. It is a system of 'managerial autonomy', not in the sense that individual managers can do what they want but in the sense that the dominant constraint on their actions is their need to negotiate co-operation from other managers – the managers of banks and other firms who are very much like themselves in outlook and background.

Let me try to spell out what are the direct and indirect consequences of this difference in financing structures between the typical Japanese and the typical Anglo-Saxon large company in a set of polar contrasts.

Mergers and acquisitions

Common, including hostile take-overs. Possibilities of acquiring and being acquired (together with the question of how to present company results in a way least damaging to share price) a major

Low concern with M&A by boards, CEOs, press. Agreed mergers not uncommon, but more likely to be inhibited by explicit concerns as to whether the 'cultures' of the merged entities will agenda item of boards, a major preoccupation of top managers and a key item of news in the financial press.

meld. Hostile takeovers exceedingly rare; frequent attempts to corner shares but nearly always with 'greenmail'[2] rather than restructuring intentions.

Managerial objectives

Above all, delivering profits to the shareholders, thereby enhancing their own claims to financial rewards within the firm and their reputation in the labour market which determines their access to alternative sources of reward. Secondary to this, fulfilment of promises they have personally given to suppliers or employees. Possibly, also, in long-established firms, pre-serving the identity and reputation of the firm.

Working for the long-term prosperity of 'the firm' (= all its employees, present and future), thereby enhancing their own reputation within the firm and hence their chances of being one of the division directors appointed to the board, then the one of their generation appointed as president, and finally the kind of president who goes on to be a respected, not disregarded, chairman and public figure, member of many good and great committees.

Indices used to measure managerial performance

Primarily share price as a combined index of earnings and growth prospects. Managers turn to the share prices in their newspapers much as academica do to citation indexes – to see how they and their friends/rivals/enemies are doing – as much as to see how much money their shares are making.

Market share, sales margins, value added per employee; growth in all these, plus total sales growth, ability to avoid any deliberate reduction of employee numbers. Of these, market share, being the most direct measure of the firm's competitiveness in the product market on which its success crucially depends, is the most important.

Disciplinary constraints on managers: accountability

For CEOs and board-level managers, a performance which loses

Managers are accountable to, and need to maintain their reputation the confidence of shareholders can lead to dismissal, either at the shareholders' AGM or by a successful takeover bidder. For lower-level managers, dismissal if they lose the confidence of their superiors.

among (a) a group of personally known individuals representing their banks and other committed shareholders and (b) their peers and juniors within the firm, on their reputation with whom their further promotion and post-retirement livelihood depends.

Social perception of the firm

Popularly, as the place where, for the moment, one earns one's living, where one might or might not also have an active and enjoyable social life and the satisfaction of interesting work, a legal entity to which one owes obligations which are time bound by the period of notice specified in the employment contract. *Academically*, 'theorizing' that popular concept, as a web of contracts, the nature of which is constrained only by law and convention, all such contracts, even those which have legal entities as contractors (the firm, a trade union) being ultimately dissolvable into the contracts of individuals.

Popularly, as a community of people, slowly renewed in composition as the old retire and new school-leavers are recruited, but having an identity and, indeed, an 'interest' which transcends, and is not simply an aggregation of, that of individual employees. Company presidents can talk, and not expect a cynical reaction when they talk, of 'the future of our great firm', in much the same way as a king or president can talk of 'the future of our great nation'. The only distinctive *academic* theorizing growing out of these popular concepts known to me is that of Aoki, in whose 'co-operative game theory' firm, managers are the arbiters of the interests of shareholders and employees.[3]

Behaviour in a recession

Strenuous efforts to maintain profitability, in order to maintain dividend and share price levels, primarily through attempts to cut

Efforts directed more towards redoubled efforts to increase sales, the prime objective being to maintain employment and money re-

[43]

costs to match fall in sales. This frequently involves redundancy dismissals, restrained in their 'ruthlessness' only by legal controls, fear of reputational effects dictated by whatever are locally current concepts of 'job rights', and fear of skill shortages in an upturn, known pejoratively as 'labour hoarding'.

wards to employees, (though the latter may well be sacrificed for the former, especially through reduced bonuses) even if this means a marked decline in profitability and, eventually, a reduction in dividend levels.

Responses to secular industry decline

Rapidly liquidate loss-making divisions, usually thereby making their workers redundant. Downsizing possibly mitigated by acquisitions of firms in growth industries; shift to higher value-added ends of traditional market.

Gradual withdrawal from declining business, compensating by internal diversification – seeking new markets and products in growth industries chosen to capitalize on existing technological skills or market expertise. Transfer of maximum possible number of employees to new activities – often undertaken in expectation of long gestation period and chosen at 'hurdle rates' of ROI well below market interest rates, even on the most optimistic estimate of eventual returns.

Wages and salaries

The distinction between the wage and the salary, as a dividing line between the 'trusted and responsible' and the 'hourly rated worker', is still the norm, in spite of much 'harmonization'. For both categories of employees, the principle of 'the rate for the job' (the market

No wage/salary distinction in the form of pay, but only between those who record and are paid for overtime and those of higher rank who do not. Relatively predictable pay-rise trajectories, levelling off after age 40. These trajectories only loosely correlate with job version) and 'equal pay for equal work' (the justice version of the same principle) have overwhelming acceptance.

functions (see above) and are at different levels and with different degrees of steepness for different 'grades' of worker, grade usually being determined by educational levels (high school leavers, arts graduates, science graduates, etc.).

Nature of the employment contract

Except for new university graduates recruited in the 'milk round' – and even for many of them – the contract is a 'job contract', specifying a certain salary/wage for a defined job function. Promotion takes place through an 'internal labour market: bids, frequently competitive bids, for vacant posts, the assumption of a new post involving the fixing of a new wage, re-contracting.

Career contracts; recruitment of most 'normal' new employees at the beginning of their work careers. There is no internal labour market; promotion is not through market processes of competition. POCADS (the personnel office career deployment system) works, as in almost any country's army or police or civil service, to 'post' employees to a succession of (a) ranks and (b) functional positions and (c) salary grades. That posting is heavily constrained by seniority as well as the merit of demonstrated performance. The three dimensions of rank, job and pay only roughly correlate. One might be given promotion on one dimension with no movement in the others.

Reward dispersion

Large.

Small.

Role of workers' unions

To maximize a worker interest seen as essentially antithetical to

Uniting the lower-ranking members of the firm (including future

[45]

that of the shareholders, to make sure that their members get the full market rate for the job and to provide them with assistance as much when they are in the market looking for a job as when they are in employment.

managers under about 35) to protect individual rights against arbitrary managers and to speak up for the claims of wages (as against investment or payments to shareholders) when decisions are made about the disposition of the firm's revenues.

Effort-inducing incentives

Mostly individual, in cash form, and short term, i.e., the reward is not too long delayed after the effort output. (Range from one week in the case of manual worker piecework to three to four years for stock option cash-ins.) Group bonuses can reward co-operativeness – helping others – as well as individual work performance, but still in the form of individual, cash payments.

Altruistic collective incentives – of the football fan type, springing from 'in-volvement' – i.e., the pleasure of seeing a firm with which one emotionally identifies doing well, may work marginally for senior long-service employers. Managers hesitate to try to evoke such sentiments for fear of the ribald cynicism which might greet such departures from the principle of the employment contract as hard-nosed arm's-length bargain.

Individual rewards are more long term – building up the reputation which (enhanced by halo-effect) may get one a crucial appointment in 20 years time, for instance. Rewards less exclusively in cash form; fast-track promotion up (a) the job function/power track and (b) the rank track can be only loosely correlated with promotion up the pay track and can carry their own intrinsic non-monetary rewards.

Altruistic collective incentives probably quite important as a determinant of effort for a high proportion of, particularly older, employees. No hesitation in seeking to evoke such sentiments.[4]

Nature of authority relations

Because the relation between manager and worker is based on explicitly adversarial contract, the organizational hierarchy is perceived more as a hierarchy of ability/licence to command obedience and co-operation than as a hierarchy of technical competence. Among technical competences, the overwhelming importance attached to dealing with financial markets tends to devalue all other forms besides the financial. (Accountants get on boards more easily than engineers.)

The sense of shared membership in the community (plus the near-guarantee of some promotion for all) modifies the adversarial nature of hierarchical relations and allows more importance to be given to technical competence when allocating authority, rather than to the possession of a steely authoritative eye. This, plus the lesser importance of financial markets, makes for boards of manufacturing companies more dominated by experts in production or product markets. More engineers than accountants.

Pension funds

Pension savings are seen as the property of the eventual recipients and the trustees of those funds have a fiduciary duty to promote their interests alone, not that of the firm which sponsors the scheme. It is held to be generally undesirable to have both present earnings and future pensions dependent on the fortunes of a single company (too many eggs in one basket).

Pension funds are frequently held within the firm, and are available to the firm as investment capital.

By How Much do the Systems Contrast?

There are two senses in which one can say that these contrasts are contrasts between different systems, rather than just different bundles of unrelated characteristics; what one might call institutional interlock and motivational sonance.

The *institutional interlock* should be rather obvious. It is because they cannot easily be unseated by shareholders that secure managers can privilege the interests of employees to the degree of giving – if not quite cast-iron, at least highly believable – guarantees of lifetime job security. And this long-term nature of the employment relation is a precondition for the strength of the social perception of the firm as a community, both through its effect on the 'commitment' of all employees to the firm and through its effect in ensuring that top managers, the fast-track promotees of a lifetime employment system, can define themselves as the 'elders' of an employee community. That perception lead to constraints on managerial exercise of power which keeps reward differentials low – which in turn strengthens the sense of community and produces the particular pattern of accountability which spurs efficient performance. It also conduces to the operation of the internal promotion system in a manner which is perceived as 'fair', that is to say, it generates a sense of managerial responsibility which ensures, by and large, that the people who receive accelerated promotion are not personal favourites but the people who have performed best (with an emphasis in the evaluation of 'performance' (following naturally from the definition of the firm as a moral community) *on the efforts* people make to use the talents they are endowed with as well as on the talents and accumulated skill and experience which they actually display). This perception of the fairness of promotion judgements is an essential precondition for the generation of trust which (a)

[48]

makes accountability work by offering the incentive of 'retaining subordinates' trust and (b) makes the long-range, slow-reward promotion system work by giving assurances that effort and cooperativeness will actually be rewarded.

Take away the financing arrangements – the shareholding pattern, the insulation from shareholder pressure to maximize short-term returns by cutting labour costs, and the invulnerability to the upheavals of take-overs – and it is easy to see how the whole institutional system could unravel.

As for *motivational sonance*, it will be fairly obvious that the institutions of the right-hand columns would work best for people who have an in-built personality propensity to get 'involved in', to identify with, groups which they join on a long-term basis. Those in the left-hand column work better for people who are individualistic not only in the sense of being self-centred in the pursuit of self-interest but also because they are prepared to recognize that others are equally self-centred and have every right to be so, and that necessary social co-operation consequently requires respect for the contracts in which the exchange relationships of self-interested parties are embodied. Proneness or non-proneness to what was called above 'altruistic collective incentives' is a crucial part of that distinction. So also is a difference in the mechanisms used to sustain the exchange relationships: greater reliance on ('making oneself vulnerable to'[5]) the partner's goodwill, in the one case, and greater reliance on the letter of the contract and formal legal redress at the margin if it is broken, on the other.

Another motivational characteristic, or behavioural disposition, relevant to adaptation to the two systems: the community firm requires patient people; short-termists find life more congenial in the property firm; the rewards for specified performance are more clearly spelt out in contract and are not so long deferred.

[49]

There is surely truth in the assertion that the community flourishes in Japan because it is a nation of groupish, patient people and the property firm in the UK because people are more individual and short termist. But before getting carried away by national character arguments, do not forget that these crude characterizations of two populations, each of many millions of people, are only observations about differences in the modes of what are probably normal-curve distributions of both patience and individualism/groupishness in both societies. There are a good many quick-buck chasing individualists in Japan whom no sensible person would trust to deliver a newspaper – all the green-mailers on the stock exchange, for example, including the one who, having failed to shock the Koito management into buying back his cornered shares at an inflated price, did the wholly un-Japanese thing of lending them to a rumbustious American, T. Boone Pickens, to see if he could do better. Equally, Britain produces quite a lot of people whose identification with, and loyalty to, their regiment, their department, their firm, far exceeds that, if not of the average Japanese, at least of those Japanese who are high on the individualism scale.

Asian Capitalism

The programme has given me the title Asian capitalism and so far I have talked exclusively about Japanese capitalism. What is the likelihood that the two will become synonymous? I recently heard the chief economist of the Deutschbank's Tokyo office forecasting the future growth of the East Asian economies, and the predominant weight they are likely to have in the total world economy in a few decades time. Japan, he said, was today an outlier, a deviant form of capitalism different from the world-dominant form. But there is a good chance that the Japanese form will spread to the rest of Asia and in consequence displace

Anglo-Saxon capitalism as the world-hegemonic form.

Maybe. I would not count on it. Michel Albert remarked that in spite of, in his view, the undoubted superiority of what he called the Rhine model of capitalism, there were more signs of Germany becoming like the United States than vice versa, and many people consider that, particularly under the effects of the longest recession in post-war history, Japan is going in the same direction – more power for the shareholders, a greater emphasis on enhancing shareholder value, diminished power for enterprise unions and a dilution of employees' rights. But the crucial question is: how far are the other high-growth economies of East Asia actually developing institutions of corporate governance, employment relations, intra-enterprise career structures, reward structures and a supporting ideology similar to that of Japan? It is a question which seems to have received very little detailed study. Remarkably, the large and detailed World Bank (1993) study says nothing whatever about enterprise structures or modes of financing, except to note the important role played by small firms and the preference of most governments for labour unions based on the enterprise rather than on industry or occupation. The research team was too preoccupied, perhaps, with its main task of mounting a rearguard action to defend the Bank's determined view that it was market forces, not government intervention, which gave East Asia its miracle growth.

With no detailed knowledge of any of the other Asian economies besides Japan, I can only present the fragments of evidence which suggest that there may, indeed, be a tendency for the large corporations emerging in East Asia to bear a distinct resemblance to the Japanese organizational form.

Korea, for instance, the most mature of the newly industrialized economic systems (NIES), has seen what were originally family-owned firms – the *chaebol* – grow into large bureaucratic

[51]

enterprises through very much the same process as occurred in Japan in the middle years of the century. In that process, power has passed increasingly to lifelong-career managers, and the inter-firm mobility of managers and engineers, which was initially very high, has diminished. One factor supporting this trend is the educational selection system. The talent-sorting function of the entrance examination system for higher education has become very similar to that of Japan: only the brightest pupils get to the top universities and only top university graduates get into the top firms, and having got into top firms they are more likely to want to make their careers there. Recently, democratization of the polity and the upsurge in labour union activity is being met by the same methods of incorporation and co-optation as were used by managers to contain labour militancy in Japan in the post-war years. They might well produce that other element of the Japanese 'community firm', legitimation of the union as the voice of the community's least powerful members – least powerful, but nevertheless recognized to be valued members of the firm community.

In China, the crucial question concerns the evolution of the state enterprises which, for all the rapid recent growth of private enterprise, joint ventures and township and village enterprises, still dominate the manufacturing sector of the economy and still have a pattern-setting role. They still share with large Japanese corporations the managerial freedom which comes from not having to satisfy shareholders, and in a recent paper Chan (1993) has looked at the prospects of these state firms as they are progressively transformed into independent corporations, evolving into Japanese-style private-sector companies. In their original form, before the economic reforms, they were already very much 'community firms'. Not only was employment guaranteed, workers who retired could even expect to be replaced by their own children: what was known as the security of the 'iron rice bowl' was

[52]

heritable. Firms often had their own housing compound, their own schools and hospitals. Come the market reforms, liberation from price constraints and price supports, tight credit and strong pressure to achieve profitability, and these community-firm aspects came under strong attack. 'Break the iron rice bowl' became the catch-all slogan of the free-market modernizers. Some of these state firms have, indeed, engineered massive reductions of employee numbers. But others have preferred the alternative strategy of sharing belt-tightening economies and trying to mobilize the co-operation of all workers to get the firm back into profit. Meanwhile China, too, has a similar educational selection system to that of Japan and Korea – the same favourable basis for the growth of bureaucracy-type career management in the elite firms.

Consider, also, the fact that the stock market seems not to be a central institution in any of these societies except perhaps Hong Kong, and even there it does not operate as the exchanges on Wall Street and London operate, to create a market in corporate control through contested takeovers.

In short, there is some evidence that there might develop a general Asian model of capitalism which bears a close resemblance to the Japanese model which I have been describing. Whether, as the Deutschbank's economist predicted, it is the model which will eclipse the Anglo-Saxon model remains to be seen.

Different in Spirit?

One final reflection. I have spoken of an Anglo-Saxon model and an Asian model, anchoring the differences in geography. But how far can the clash or the competition between them be seen as a clash of values or of ideologies – a clash, perhaps, between

[53]

what one might, borrowing from Max Weber, call the Protestant Individualistic model and the Confucian Communitarian model? I would not suggest that Japanese firms got to be the way they were because the Japanese were convinced by Confucian doctrine, any more than Weber, except occasionally and incautiously, was suggesting that Western capitalism got to be the way it was because of the teachings of Calvin. The process, rather, goes something like this. Certain social attitudes and values widely diffused in ancient China were codified in Confucian doctrine, substantially recoded a thousand years later in the Sung version of Confucianism, subsequently much strengthened by that codification and by the ritual and educational institutions which were developed in its name, and later diffused, by explicit teaching, throughout China, Korea, Japan, Vietnam and in the Chinese diaspora which plays such a prominent role in the economies of Thailand, Malaysia and Indonesia. The question is whether these attitudes and values are in some way consonant with the Asian model of capitalism in the way that protestant individualism is consonant with the values of Anglo-Saxon capitalism. Even an amateur at cultural analysis like myself can make out what seems to me a good case for saying: probably yes.

First, the emphasis on life as being about the fulfilment of duty rather than the pursuit of happiness conduces to acceptance of the sort of heavy commitment and restriction of choice options which lifetime membership in a Japanese firm entails.

Second, there is what one might call a 'productivist' emphasis in Confuciamism; producing goods and services is more worthy than merely making money by clever arbitrage. In traditional Confucian society the prestige ranking of the 'four orders' – the governing literati, the peasant, the artisan and the merchant – it was the merchant who came at the bottom. His essential role in getting goods from the producer to the consumer was always liable to be subverted by the temptations of speculation. In a

Confucian society the financial sector should serve as the handmaiden of the real economy; not, as increasingly in Anglo-Saxon economies, the other way round.

Third, there is a curious balance between hierarchy and equality. Confucian societies are not democracies, but meritocracies. Every man and woman may be born with equal rights to consideration as human beings, but there is no pretence that every man and woman is born with equal judgement, equal skill, equal rights to take decisions on which the health of society depends. Hierarchy, and the concentration of decision-making power in the hands of those who are most skilled and gifted, i.e., qualified managers, is inevitable and natural. But skilled and gifted also means having a refined moral sense; it means that responsible officials and responsible managers should not abuse their power. They should exercise benevolence, show consideration towards their less-gifted brothers, live modestly and not enrich themselves excessively at those fellow-citizens' expense.

These ideals, like any other ideals, can be used as a hypocritical cover for repression and exploitation. But they can also, when taken seriously as a morally restraining code of behaviour, produce the sort of co-operation which secures the kind of rapid growth, and relative equality of distribution of the proceeds of growth, for which the East Asian economies are noted. There are people in Japan who clearly articulate these ideals as the values underlying their form of capitalism, and speak of them as something of which they can be proud and which they should consciously seek to preserve. There are also many others – particularly the economists trained in American graduate schools and the bond-traders and other eager participants in the global financial economy – who see these ideals and their institutional embodiment in the Japanese corporation as evidence of Japan's backward-looking rejection of the principles of liberty and efficiency embodied in the universal ideal of the free market economy. The latter, claiming the support of science – rational

[55]

social science as the solvent of soft-headed traditionalism – seem at the moment to have the upper hand in the ideological debate, although not, yet, in business practice. Whether they finally win the day will probably indeed depend, as the Deutschbank's economist suggested, on whether the Japanese model does eventually become a more general East Asian, post-Confucian, form of capitalism.

Notes

1 Sales margins (operating profit/total sales) varied between 3.2 per cent (1985) and 5.1 per cent (1980) in Japanese manufacturing during the 1980s (EPA, 1992, *Keizai Yoran*, p. 102), between 12.8 per cent (1982) and 15.5 per cent (1988) in the US (Standard and Poor's Industrial 400 (1993): *Standard and Poor's Analysts Handbook*, official series, annual edn.) Dividends plus directors' bonuses as a percentage of sales fluctuated between 0.5 per cent and 0.6 per cent in Japan, 2.0 per cent and 2.3 per cent (dividends only) in the US (same sources.)

  A similar difference between British and German firms is found by Henk de Jong. He compares the division of net added value, as between government (taxation), capital and labour of the 23 German and the 27 British firms numbered among the EC's 100 largest firms. The figures for 1991 were, respectively, 7, 5 and 89 per cent for the German, and 11, 21 and 68 per cent for the British. Jong, H. W. de, 'European capitalism: Between freedom and social justice', to appear in *Review of Industrial Organization*, pp. 399–419.

2 For details of share-cornering operations, see Sheard, P. (1991): The economics of interlocking shareholding in Japan. *Ricerche Economiche* , 1991, 45, pp. 428–9.

3 For a sample of left-hand column theory, see Kay (1993): *Foundations of Corporate Success: How Business Strategies Add Value*, Oxford: Oxford University Press, and the work of theorists such as Oliver Hart on which it draws. For Aoki's work, see Aoki, M.

(1984): *The Cooperative-game Theory of the Firm*. Oxford: Clarendon Press.

4 There is by now a considerable economics literature on Japanese firms' promotion system which seeks to model the way they are 'rational'. Being entirely individualistic, as all such models have to be calculable, let alone respectable, they have no place for – in fact are often explicitly motivated by the desire to deny the importance of – what are called here 'altruistic collective incentives'. A survey of such models, and of their inadequacies, may be found in Itoh, H. (1994): Japanese HRM and incentive theory. In M. Aoki and R. Dore (eds), *The Japanese firm: Sources of competitive strength*, Oxford: Clarendon Press. See also Odagiri, H. (1990): *Growth through competition: competition through growth: Strategic management and the economy in Japan*. Oxford: Clarendon Press.

5 I owe this suggestive formulation of the nature of 'trust' to a paper by Edward Lorenz.

References

Albert, M. (1991): *Capitalisme Contre Capitalisme*, Paris: Seuil (trans. 1993 as *Capitalism Against Capitalism*. London: Whurr.

Albert, M. (1993): *Capitalism vs. Capitalism*. New York: Four walls Eight windows.

Chan, A. (1993): Chinese enterprise reforms: convergence with the Japanese model?, Australian National University. mimeo.

ERT (1995): Communication to the CAG, June 1995: *European competitiveness – the five benchmarks for growth and jobs*. Brussels: European Round Table.

World Bank (1993): *The East Asian Miracle: Growth and Public Policy*.

[57]

3

The European Corporation

H. W. de Jong

The Concept of the Corporation

What do we mean when we discuss corporate enterprise? Obviously not the rank and file of firms and companies that form the bulk of every country's enterprise system. The thousands and thousands of small, personally run businesses, however important they may be, do not constitute the corporate business world and, although nearly every corporate firm of importance has evolved out of small beginnings, it has achieved its position by means of some mutative change(s). Neither do we restrict the concept to the legal form under which corporate enterprise operates. Legal forms differ between time and place and, even at a given moment in a particular country, the legal structures of large enterprises may differ; for example, of the hundred largest German corporations in 1992, only 69 were Aktiengesellschaften (AG), 15 were Gesellschaften mit beschränkter Haftung (GmbH), some 11 were clothed in one of the varieties of the Kommanditgesellschaft (KG) or Offene Handelsgesellschaft (OHG), and five had other forms (Monopol-kommission, 1994, p. 201). The legal form of enterprise may be a factor of great importance; it may enable firms to do things which otherwise would be impossible, or it can restrict them in their operations, but it does not, by itself, make for economic significance.

[58]

Economic aspects relate to size, space and time; all three have been rather neglected by traditional economic theory though neither by historians nor by industrial organization experts or regional economists. Conceptualizing the business corporation has proven to be a difficult job and various theories do exist. Teece has discussed several of them in an interesting article (Teece, 1991). But it seems to me that his solution, emphasizing the characteristics of economizing by means of internalizing economic activity in a hierarchical system (the transaction cost approach), the development of cumulative, organizational skills and the path dependency of learning (being mostly irreversible and constrained also in a forward sense) is not entirely satisfactory.

First, no distinction is made between a firm or company and a corporation. The criteria mentioned pertain as well to the former as to the latter, though most firms are not corporations.

Second, a factor which merits attention is the element of control, by means of which the economic organization – whether a firm or a corporate entity – is steered by the ultimate decision makers. In a preliminary approach, the corporation may be defined as a group of legally separate firms which are under joint economic control. Control in organizations entails the setting of goals, the adoption of methods or ways of behaviour and the valuation of the results achieved.

What distinguishes a corporation from other types of companies or firms (though both terms may quite innocently sometimes be used to describe corporations, for example the 'Philips company') is a double criterium.

First, the *transcendental nature* of a corporation, that is, its characteristics of transcending the normal or average size of firms in a given period, of transcending limited relevant markets and thus expanding into wider economic space than other firms do and, finally, the transcending of subjective time in the sense that it continues to exist beyond the life of the owner–founder.

[59]

These characteristics are interrelated and should be cumulatively satisfied if we are to speak of a corporation. Thus the corporation is a sizeable, multi-market, multi-period organization, and this criterium applies as well to the fifteenth-century Medici Holding Corporation, the seventeenth-century Dutch East India Company, as to twentieth-century Royal Dutch-Shell or Siemens.

Second, an additional criterium is *meta-control*, by which is meant the ownership and the steering of the organization in an indirect, and sometimes hardly visible way. Remote control would be another term to describe what is meant: the leading people set goals and pull levers, through which forces start to operate which directly or indirectly steer behaviour to some desired result. It is clear that remote control extends power substantially; but it causes as well as is caused in a mutual process by the transcendental aspects of size, space and time. Such control need not be hierarchical in a vertical sense.

Remote control can operate in various ways, both with respect to ownership and in relation to the behaviour of subordinates. The classic example in the first domain is the pyramid structure through which a small top capital controls a very large base. The holding-company structure, dating back to the fourteenth century as de Roover (1966, p. 81) has convincingly shown, offers a variety of vertical solutions in a similar vein.

Horizontally, a set of *n* diverse companies, each having a different group of owners, would be a corporation if they have one common owner with a managerial role, even if that were a minority owner. Such structures, which can easily evolve into networks, are in reality very old; they too began to appear in the fourteenth century and constituted groups of companies in which the corporation was difficult to demarcate (Origo, 1963, p. 112).

It is likewise with respect to the federated structure of business corporations. The Dutch East and West Indian companies of the seventeenth and eighteenth centuries were of the latter type. The boards of gentlemen of both corporations

[60]

exerted remote control through laying down guidelines as well as taking fixed decisions, communicated by a permanent secretary-general to the various regional 'chambers', which constituted the operating arm. However, because these regional organizations were represented on the board and shared in the results according to a fixed key, those corporations were a curious mixture of federated policy formation and decentralized policy execution. In modern times, both Shell and Unilever, as well as other corporate groups, have kept decisive elements of such federated structures. Japanese *Keiretsu*-organizations are another prominent example of the method of exerting remote control; some insiders pretend to say that they are corporations (Miyashita and Russell, 1996, pp. 197–8), the primary purpose being to stabilize economic performance in unruly times (de Jong, 1971, pp. 165–9).

Thus, the transcendental nature of its operations as well as its remote control mechanisms determine whether one may call a group of companies a business corporation, even though it may assume different structures. Negatively, it has to be underlined that the owner–capital base – *il corpo della compagnia* or, in the plural, *il corpo delle compagnie*[1] – is not a decisive criterion, however important it may be in itself.

Not only do many European corporations have different ownership structures of their subsidiaries; also, the stockholders, having entrusted the capital to the corporation, share decision power with respect to crucial issues of control with managers, labour representatives and the banks. Thus, split-ups of profitable corporations, as occurred in recent years with ATT, ICI, Kodak and others in the Anglo-Saxon domain, are difficult to realize in Continental Europe. Failing firms may be more easily restructured to find a solution both for their debts and for their viable parts. However, one has to distinguish between horizontally and vertically structured corporations; the latter ones disintegrate more easily under mounting pressures because it is

[61]

quality, cost and speed that determine the decision to integrate or not, whereas the horizontal relationships provide security and serve expansionary purposes (Miyashita and Russell, 1996, pp. 205–6).

Corporate History (1).
The Commercial Revolution

Europe is, naturally, the mother of the business corporation, as its birth and growth has paralleled general economic expansion. As the latter started in the thirteenth century (de Roover, 1942) with the so-called 'commercial revolution', we should not be astonished to find in that century the beginnings of corporate enterprise. The reasons are to be found in a cumulation of new techniques which raised managerial control to such an extent that the personally travelling merchant became superfluous. He was replaced by the sedentary merchant, who established agencies or partnerships elsewhere, run by factors and partners. Such techniques were maritime insurance, the letter of payment or bill of exchange, good methods of bookkeeping to straighten the accounts between persons residing in different cities, culminating in double-entry bookkeeping, the formation of durable partnerships, education in letterwriting by Latin schools and universities, etc.

This commercial revolution meant the elimination of the great European fairs of Champagne, where merchants from Southern and Northern Europe had traditionally met to exchange their specialties. It was the Italian merchant – from Genoa, Venice, Florence, Siena, Pisa and other cities – who seized the opportunities and created business corporations which were to dominate European interregional trade for the next three centuries. With the exception of the northern rim, which was the domain of the Hanseatics, the Italians proved superior, so much so that the Flemish and British traders had to retreat to production and brokerage functions in their home cities. One would go amiss by interpreting these developments in terms of transaction cost economics, for the one market which was superseded – the Champagne fairs – was replaced by several new ones at London, Bruges, Avignon and Geneva, for example. The new business organization destroyed one type of market and created another type (an additional factor was the rise of the Florentine cloth industry).

Italian company development was of two sorts: in the maritime cities, such as Genoa, Venice, Pisa, Amalfi, but also in Marseilles and Barcelona, sea voyages gave rise to partnerships, through which the risks could be distributed, also for the prominent merchants. At the same time, liability was limited by means of reducing the individual shares per partnership and the taking part in many of them.

Wealthy people thus could participate in many partnerships and people of smaller means at least in one or two. In this way, important capitals were mobilized which could be entrusted to a manager, responsible for the ship and goods, as well as foreign sales and purchases. The legal form was a series of maritime loans contractually laid down with notaries and guaranteed both for the capital and the interest by the borrowing shipper and/ or other shipowners. Those guarantees were obviously not meant against 'acts of God': shipwreck, robbery, piracy and similar events. In order to secure a shipowner's own interest in the venture, the general rule which prevailed in all Mediterranean trade was a fixed distribution of the profits: 75 per cent to capital and 25 per cent to the managerial labour of the shipper. In addition, the manager faced penalties if he did not live up to his obligations, whereas the owners had to prove the calamities. Such partnerships had different names in various cities: *commenda*, *colleganza* (Venice), *accomenda* (Ligurian coast and Marseilles), *colonna* (Amalfi), etc. The basic form could be varied and also be

[63]

linked with a network of merchant–agent relationships (Kedar, 1976, pp. 25–7).

It is interesting to note why Venice did not develop big corporations like the Tuscan cities, although there were enough wealthy people. The state supplied, since the middle of the fourteenth century, the great merchant galleys nearly all of which were built at the arsenal of the republic, and when the senators decided that a fleet should sail, they stipulated the route, the crew, freight rates and other variables. Thus the operation of the galleys for a specific voyage was awarded to the highest bidder at auction. He became galley master or patron (Lane, 1953, p. 94). Investments in a fleet of galleys, such as those sailing for Flanders or Alexandria, surpassed the resources of even the richest families. Their cargoes might likewise exceed individual family wealth. Families thus had no incentives to join together in durable corporations, owning ships and stores, 'because the government required merchant operators to charter the galleys a-new for each voyage. Since the state did so much, the famed Venetian galley voyages created no need for any private business institution having either the longevity of the corporation or the large capital and the large powers of command which are organized in the corporation' (Lane and Riemerson, 1953, p. 99).

In addition the state took measures restraining *commenda*-type organizations, so that they dwindled in later periods. An Act of 1324 prohibited citizens from investing in maritime trade a sum exceeding capital limits linked to forced loans; it was intermittently enforced even after 1360 and hastened the demise of the *commenda* contract (Kedar, 1976, pp. 27–8). Likewise, *commenda* contracts were changed in such a way that the investing partner could force the travelling partner to bear half the losses.

In contrast, partners in Tuscan cities, supplying both capital and management, founded *compagnie*. Many of them arose out of

[64]

families; frequently they also consisted of men unrelated by blood.

Companies were established by contract, which contained as main points:

- the capital of the firm, the contributions of partners and the rules governing the distribution of the profits;
- the duration of the firm, mostly between two and 12 years.

However, these relatively short periods were stipulated to give partners the possibility to opt out at the end: in practice, many companies continued for a long time, such as those of the Bardi or the Peruzzi which lasted over 70 years, or the Medici Holding which existed for nearly a century.

Companies could be swelled by deposits of outsiders at fixed interest, sums which were called *il fuori corpo* or *sopra corpo*; but a higher-level structure was reached by the formation of several companies at different places by different people, except for the Florentine or Pratoese *capo*. The latter was the uniting element and the person or group of men taking the strategic decisions. In this way the first steps towards the holding company structure were made by Datini (Origo, 1963, p. 112), soon followed by the Medici (de Roover, 1966, pp. 77–86). Industrial production, trade, finance and banking were combined into European-wide corporations of outstanding dimensions.

If the Tuscan entrepreneurs evaded the drawbacks of the organizational forms of the maritime cities, they had other disadvantages which discredited them in due time. Two were of particular importance.

First, for all their size and international spread, they remained personally or family-led corporations, dependent on personalities who are mortals, have ambitions (or not) and follies, and have their different styles of leadership. The practical identity of *il capo* and *il corpo della compagnia* in some cases meant that the

[65]

corporation was vulnerable to decline. Thus the Datini firm ended with the death of Francesco, its founder, while the Medici bank, when it was seized in 1494, was practically bankrupt due to the failing leadership of Lorenzo il Magnifico and his general manager Sassetti (de Roover, 1966, pp. 358–77). Somewhat differently, the Bardi and Peruzzi corporations failed, partly as a result of quarrels at the top in moments of financial troubles (the 1340s), whereas action saved the Alberti from impending doom (de Roover, 1974, p. 75).

Second, the Tuscan corporations did not have limited liability, a feature which is a cornerstone of a corporation's durability, size and efficiency.

It was the Dutch and the British who reaped the full advantages of corporate organization. Whereas the *commenda* faded out in Venice, it grew to private and public corporations in Holland and Britain. The essential explanation is the confluence of rising European demand for bulk goods (wood, grain, metals and salt), new techniques for building other types of ships and improved corporate organization. Techniques, developed between 1450–60 of joining the ship's planks by means of fitting instead of overlaying them, greatly increased ship strength and size; consequently, the three-masted, full-rigged ship replaced the one-masted cog. Somewhat later, the flute or fly-ship, combining speed, stability and low personnel cost in relation to volume was invented at Hoorn in 1595; as a result, the representative size of sea-going merchant ships rose from 100–150 ton to 800–1000 ton between 1460 and 1750. Corporate organization was greatly facilitated by reduction in the size of the capital parts (1:64, 1:128, etc.), limited liability, anonymity of shareholders and transferability in a freely accessible market. Figure 3.1 illustrates the principle.

Total revenue R from some particular trade rises with increasing scale of operations. Costs C also rise, but at a decreased rate because of economies of scale, made possible by

Figure 3.1 The corporate advantage

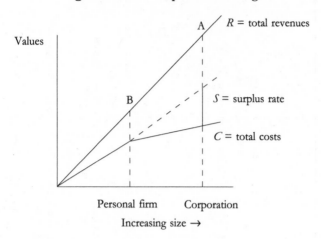

using larger ships or faster ships (the flute ship as from 1595, for example). Now, a private corporation or a public one, by means of spreading risks and amassing participations from several merchants, can reach revenue point A on the curve R, whereas a personally run business, at the same point in time, can only achieve point B. The premium – or corporate rent – due to the corporate structure is to be measured by the S part of the net added value of the corporation, and which the personal business cannot gain. This part, therefore, represents excess profits, resulting from risk sharing related to scale economies, which can be reinvested in the next period, either in the same business or in some other. In this way, temporary profit leads gained by the corporation are converted into accumulated capital, the increasing supply of which drives down the rate of interest. In the fourteenth century the rate of interest in Amsterdam was 8½ per cent; throughout the fifteenth century, and especially during the second half, the interest rate fell to 6 per cent and by 1497 it was

[67]

Table 3.1 Profits of major corporations in earlier times

Name	Location	Period in existence	Profits (as % of capital)	During period	Remarks
Grosze Ravens-burger Gesell-schaft	S. Germany	c.1380–1530	6.8–7.5	1497–1514	Previously higher
Welser/Vöhler	Augsburg	1498–1614	8.9	1502–17	Probably understated
Fugger	Augsburg	1450–1645	over 15.0	1500–20	Heyday of the corporation
Medici Holding	Florence	1397–1494	16.8–25.9	1397–1450	Averages for the periods 1397–1420, 1421–35, 1436–51
Dutch East India Company	Amsterdam	1602–1796	15.0–55.0.	1640–1780	Between 1650–1730: > 30%; afterwards declining
Dutch West India Company	Amsterdam	1621–1791	Very high to Nil Nil	1621–42 1674–86	In other periods only losses
Hudson Bay Company	London	1670–1821, 1822–present	Hardly any profits 8–10 4	1670–1718 1718–82 1783–1821	In 1821 merger with North West Company

Sources: Kellenbenz (1977), pp. 187, 195, 282; de Roover (1966), pp. 47, 50, 55, 61, 66–9); de Jong (1995, p. 223); net value added on total assets, calculated from de Korte (1983, p. 70); den Heyer (1994, pp. 97–8, 185); Newman (1986, pp. 466–74)

[68]

down to 5 per cent (Posthumus 1953, p. 58). In the next two centuries it further declined to 2½–4 per cent (Israel, 1989, pp. 78–9).

In Britain a similar decline occurred a century later when political stabilization and institutional renovation was achieved.[2] Expansion during the eighteenth century was accompanied by a rate of interest which declined from 8–10 per cent in 1680–90, to 3–4 per cent at the time of Walpole and Pelham (about 1750). In our time, the Japanese have demonstrated the same nexus. The advantages of low interest rates for the economy at large need not be dwelt on.

The performance of the earlier corporations

It is naturally difficult to get a view on the profitability of the earlier European corporations. Documents have been lost or are only incompletely available; calculations are problematic because of the capital base, profits may have been overstated or understated, as Lucas Rem, a high official in the Welser company, said when he had departed the firm (Kellenbenz, 1977, p. 195).

Table 3.1 nevertheless assembles some data on profits achieved in particular periods by some of the large corporations of earlier times. It has to be kept in mind that these firms were corporations in our sense, existing for long periods, transcending their domestic markets and carrying out business at least throughout Europe and being of large size. They were conglomerates having activities in trade, mining, manufacturing, finance and sometimes banking (such as the Medici and Fuggers). Also, because of their international spread, these corporations had to practise some system of remote control, which for long periods did work very well, but, in the end, because of laxity and fraud, contributed to their downfall (Medici, Welser). In any case, these corporations do show some roughly similar patterns in profitability: after an initial period of low profitability the corporation has periods of high profits (ranging from a few decades to over a century) and a tendency of the profitability rate (the curve showing the percentage on total assets) to decline which demonstrates the operation of Menger's Law, i.e. that an innovative start, which establishes successfully a monopoly or dominant position, issues into competitive markets through price declines forced by competitors. In the case of the Dutch East India Company, the innovative feature was the corporate joint-stock form with limited liability and transferable shares (Steensgaard, 1982, pp. 239–44).

The British East India Company, which was founded in 1600, had a similar structure but was much smaller. It had a capital of £70,000 as against £600,000 for its great rival. This corporation lost its monopoly in 1654 through the interference of Cromwell; it was chartered anew in 1693 and had its most prosperous period during the middle of the eighteenth century, after which it, too, languished and was ended in 1856. Unfortunately, the figures provided by Chaudhuri (1993, pp. 78–80) do not enable me to calculate profitability. The Hudson Bay Company was established as a joint-stock company in London in 1670, although printed share certificates were not issued until 1863 (Newman, 1986, p. 111).

Corporate History (2).
The Industrial Revolution

The pattern, outlined in the preceding section, was repeated when the industrial revolution started in the eighteenth century. Initially, firms were small; at most they had a few hundred workpeople. After half a century of industrial growth a few larger firms began to appear, but apart from everything else they were not corporations in the sense we have defined them in the beginning: neither in space nor time did they transcend the limits of ordinary firms and, as to size, the industrial companies could not stand comparison to the big trading corporations. Whereas the Dutch East India company employed between 25,000 and 35,000 people during the eighteenth century,[3] its French and British rivals had between 5,000 and 10,000 men on their payrolls, and even smaller trading corporations like the Dutch West India Company, the Danish East India Company and the Hudson Bay Company, had 1,000–2,000.[4] In contrast, the two largest textile firms in Britain indirectly employed 4,000 to 7,000 workers, namely including a dominant share of outworking weavers;[5] the majority of textile manufacturers employed only a few hundred workers well into the nineteenth century.[6] Occasionally some mining firms like Coal Company d'Anzin could employ 4,000 men and 12 steam engines,[7] but these were exceptions, even in industries like iron, chemicals, machinework and ship-building where the separation between home work and the business had always existed, unlike textiles (Landes, 1969, pp. 120–1). A large establishment, like the British naval arsenal at Chatham employed 'upwards of a thousand men, all of them carefully assigned and supervised' (Landes, 1969, p. 120).

It was only during the second half of the nineteenth century and after the passage of the joint-stock company acts in Britain (1856–62), France (1863–7) and Germany (1843–71), that joint-stock companies generally eased the way for large-scale industrial, transport and financial firms (Landes, 1969, p. 199; Kellenbenz, 1981, pp. 58, 80–2). In separate sectors of industry, such as railroads, sea transport, mining, canal and bridge construction, the joint-stock firm with limited liability ran ahead of events driven mainly by largely increased capital requirements; but governments severely controlled the process for fears of speculation and abuse (Freedeman, 1979, pp. 27–47, 66–99, 123; Kellenbenz, 1981, pp. 76–9; Bösselmann, 1939, tables 199–201).

Consequently, the first half of the nineteenth century saw only a slight increase in Aktiengesellschaften in Prussia, and none at all in France.

Table 3.2 makes a comparison between both countries. It should be remembered that France at the time was a much larger (populous) nation than Prussia. The time periods do not completely overlap, but that is of marginal importance, because only ten AGs were founded in Prussia between 1800–20, and French approvals during the 1850s fell back somewhat in comparison with the 1830s and 1840s.

Only four broad sectors were responsible for respectively three-fifths and three-quarters of the total number of incorporations, and for over 90 per cent of the capitalizations. Railway firms account for the lion's share, with banks and insurance companies in a second position. This roughly comparable picture for both countries shows (1) that policy with respect to incorporation was very reticent, and (2) that manufacturing industry and commerce hardly took part in the movement.

This cautiousness on the part of the authorities was connected with the heart of the matter: *il corpo della compagnia*, for which founders of firms and investors only accepted limited liability in cases of Soc. Anonymes (SAs) and AGs. Governments and their advisors (such as the *Conseil d'Etat* in France) simply mistrusted the concept of corporate capital with limited liability on the part of the owners, and only hesitatingly approved of proposals where economic developments forced them, as in the cases of railways, banks, insurance companies, mines and metallurgical firms. Even then there were severe tests with lengthy delays.

Proposals were tested with respect to sectors (public utilities: yes; manufacturing and commerce, mostly: no); size of the capital (absolutely and relatively), the structure of the capital (fixed and working capital); number of shareholders and value of the shares; the valuation of non-liquid assets and the share of sunk costs in the capitalization; fears of gigantic enterprises as

[72]

Table 3.2 Approvals of joint-stock companies
(per cent distribution)

Sectors	France (1821–1859)		Prussia (1800–1850)	
	Number	Capitalization	Number	Capitalization
Railways	9.4	72.9	22.0	60.7
Banks and insurance	27.5	11.6	29.7	25.5
Transport (other than railways)	14.4	7.8	15.3	2.1
Mining and metallurgy	11.2	7.6	11.0	9.0
Total four sectors	62.5	93.9	78.0	97.3
Number of firms	501	100.0	118	100.0

Sources: Freedeman (1979, pp. 28, 68, 82); Bösselmann (1939, p. 200)

well as of small firms with few stockholders; the diversity of operations (mostly suspect); the presence of debts and mortgages; the solvency of promoters, etc. Conservatism is a general explanation for the reticence, mixed with fears about speculation, fraud and the riskiness of future operations. In many cases the appointment of a government commissioner to exercise surveillance over operations and the submission of balance sheets to the ministry were inserted in a company's charter before approval was obtained (mostly to no effect, see Freedeman, 1979, pp. 127–9). Such fears went back to the histories of John Law's schemes in the 1720s and similar scandals. In addition, it was pointed out that Britain's superior manufacturing firms could do without limited joint-stock firms and that Continental adoption of the corporate capital concept, independent of the owners, would only serve to increase the risks. Such reasoning is also substantiated by table 3.2: the 'approved' sectors were oriented towards domestic markets.

The explosion of incorporations, after the 'triumph of free incorporation' (Freedeman, 1979, ch. 7), expressed in the joint-stock acts of the 1850s and 1860s, demonstrates that the previous policy had a retarding effect on the growth of the European corporation.

In France, the number of existing SAs rose from a few hundred at the passage of the 1869 Act to 6,300 in 1898 and about double that amount in 1909, although at an irregular rate, depending on the economic cycle (Clapham, 1966, pp. 396–400). The German figures likewise rose from slightly over 300 in 1870 to 3,700 in 1896 and 5,222 in 1909. To these AGs, some 16,500 should be added for the GmbHs – a limited liability corporation with more restricted obligations than the AG, created under the law of 1893 to facilitate the incorporation of medium-sized enterprise. But Britain still led the way with 46,000 limited companies (exclusive of railways) in 1909 (Clapham, 1966, pp. 399–400).

At the same time, invested share capitals increased still more strongly, for example by 203 per cent in Germany between 1886 and 1909, as against a rise of 144 per cent in the number of AGs testifying to the increased capital intensity of industrial enter-prise. Also, the movement was no longer confined to railways and banks/insurance companies, but spread to manufacturing and commerce. It was only at the turn of the century that the largest European firms came to surpass the earlier Dutch East India Company in terms of employment: Krupp, 70,000 (in 1909); Stinnes, 38,000; the Haniel and Gelsenkirchen companies, with 42,000 and 37,000 workpeople (Harbutt-Dawson, 1912, pp.

[74]

92–5) and, in Britain, the Fine Cotton Spinners and Doublers with 30,000 workers (Hannah, 1983, p. 22).

This explosion of joint-stock company foundations before 1914 had immediate consequences as well as influences which made themselves felt throughout the twentieth century. It is true that two world wars and the inter-war political and economic troubles had substantial effects on European corporate enterprise but, in retrospect, one might hold that the following salient features, present at the beginning of the century, also characterize the second half of the age.

- The association of capitals in business corporations had accommodated the technical progress which has been the hallmark of the industrial revolution. In turn, both have jointly given rise to the enormous increase in output, once markets for new products and production processes were developed. Already, before 1914 and throughout the rest of the century, this has meant the mutual penetration of other European countries by the large corporations: through exports and imports, foreign establishments, affiliated companies, mergers and takeovers, agreements and other 'interests'. Large firms have become 'Europeanized' to an extent far surpassing political integration.
- The growth of output and markets has severely increased the intensity of competition, directly through downward pressure on prices and, indirectly, by increasing the presence in each other's markets. The combination of technology and joint-stock has sustained and fostered the operation of Menger's Law, that is, that new markets, initially characterized by monopoly and/or tight oligopoly in a restricted domain, widen towards great size, many competitors and fierce price competition. In sector after sector the pattern was repeated. In the pre-1914 European chemicals markets, for example, prices fell to one-third, one-fourth or one-

[75]

seventh of their previous levels within periods ranging from one decade to 40 or 50 years (Hohenberg, 1967, p. 110).

In the post-war period airline passenger transport receipts in dollar cents per passenger-mile fell from 28 cents in 1960 to 13 cents in 1995. The phenomenon is a general one (see Klepper and Graddy, 1990).

- The reaction to more intensive competition was the combination movement which took various forms: cartel agreements, division of markets, fixing prices and allotting quotas sometimes verging on central control as in many syndicates; mergers between large firms and takeovers, mostly of smaller enterprises by the large; vertical integration, especially in the iron and steel trades, coal mining and between firms in both sectors.

The combination movement occurred in four waves, namely from 1890–1910 (first wave), between 1919–29/30 (second wave), between 1960–73 (third wave) and from 1983–90 (fourth wave). After a decline in mergers, takeovers and joint ventures in the years 1991–3, there was a renewed rise in 1994 and 1995, but it is premature to speak of another wave.

Corporate Size and Structure in the Twentieth Century

Increasing size has been a general feature of European business during the present century, but it would be interesting to establish whether the largest firms have grown more or less than proportionally. Unfortunately, statistics to provide an answer to this question are not readily available for Europe as a whole. However, the tendencies displayed in some of the larger European countries can probably be generalized. Before the Second World War there was first a rise during the period up to 1930, followed by a standstill in the 1930s and 1940s. Concentration again increased at a rapid rate in the 1950s and 1960s, but roughly speaking stabilized in the 1970s and 1980s. Thus, in the UK the share of the 100 largest firms in the net output of manufacturing industry rose from 16 per cent in 1909 to 27 per cent in 1953 and 41 per cent in 1972 (Prais, 1976, pp. 4, 213), but has risen no further since then. According to Hannah (1995, table 2, p. 58) it even declined by four percentage points. In Germany, the concentration survey of 1964 reported a substantial rise in the share of the 50 and 100 largest firms in mining and manufacturing, but the Monopolies Commission changed the approach substantially since it first published similar statistics in the early 1970s (Monopolkommission, 1973/1975, pp. 108–9); in its latest report (Monopolkommission, 1994, p. 81) it shows a stagnation in the share of the 100 largest firms of slightly over 35 per cent between 1977 and 1991. The French concentration rate rose from 10 per cent in 1981 to 36 per cent in 1990 (Hannah, 1995, p. 58). Finally, within Europe as a whole (counting the original six EC member states plus the UK), the share of the 100 largest firms against the GDP increased from 21 per cent in 1961 to 29 per cent in 1977, after which there was a stabilization at about 28 per cent in 1989 and 1993 (see de Jong, 1993, p. 6).

These tendencies, making for a general increase in the share of the largest corporations – though at an irregular rate for different time periods and for different countries – are documented also for the United States and Japan (Hannah, 1995, table 2), but the Japanese case differs from those of the Western countries in that the level achieved in 1990 was markedly lower (21 per cent) and the tendency since 1947 has been flat (Hannah's share of 28 per cent in 1946 was before the break-up of the *zaibatsu*).

What about the composition of the group of the largest

European firms? Did the corporations who were in that group during earlier periods remain there or were they replaced by other ones? The calculation of survival rates for various sub-groups in table 3.3 shows that the largest 12 firms have increased their survival rate appreciably: from two-thirds in the 1960s to a 100 per cent in the 1980s. The lower-sized sub-groups have lost in the survivor race: every ten-year period or so, the numbers 25–100 lose 3 out of 10 of the previously existing group through failure, takeover or a dropping out of the group through slow growth or decline. Rank mobility indicators point into the same direction (de Jong, 1993, p. 9). They are on about the same level as those of the US and Japan and have generally increased since the middle 1970s.

It would seem therefore that European big business is, comparatively speaking, sufficiently competitive: a statement which is also supported by the evidence concerning the share of Europe's largest firms in the world total as enumerated by Fortune since 1962. That share rose from 29.4 per cent in 1962 to 30.4 per cent in 1982 and 33.1 per cent in 1992; also, the relative size of the large European firms as compared to US firms has systematically increased during the past decades, although Japanese corporations have drawn level to both the US and

Table 3.3 Survival rates of the largest corporations

Size class	Periods 1962–1971	1973–1981	1981–1993
1–12	0.66	0.75	1.00
1–25	0.68	0.67	0.72
1–50	0.80	0.82	0.70
1–100	0.74	0.84	0.69

Calculations based on sales, as recorded in the Fortune 500 list

Table 3.4 Specialization and diversification of large firms (100 largest companies per country in %)

Firms	France	UK	Italy	Germany
Specialized and dominant				
in 1950	63	75	54	61
in 1970	48	40	43	44
Diversified				
in 1950	33	23	43	32
in 1970	42	54	52	38
Conglomerate				
in 1950	4	2	3	7
in 1970	10	6	5	18

Sources: Channon (1974); Dyas (1972); Pavan (1972); Dyas and Thanheiser (1976)

European giants. Clearly, future competition is a triangular contest.

I refrain from discussing the tendencies in the internal organization of corporations in post-war decades. The subject is a vast one and, moreover, the literature is soon dated by fashions and events. Most large European firms in the immediate post-war period were functionally organized, mostly because of their specialization in one product class. When competition increased and product markets matured in the ensuing decades large firms in all countries diversified into other product classes, although probably to a lesser extent than in the US (table 3.4; also compare the essays in Chandler and Daems, 1980).

Many firms created multi-divisional structures in their organizations and for a time this was seen as a belated response to more advanced American structures (Chandler, 1977; Channon, 1974, pp. 236–46). However, the 1980s saw a reverse movement, with decentralization into business units, being responsible for productivity and profits, and 'lean management' as well as concentration on so-called core activities taking over. Nowadays, technology as a base for quality products and 'long-leash' management are increasingly stressed, as are human resource management tasks (Henzler, 1994, pp. 87–125). It appears therefore that European management has come to understand that the creation of net added value is the supreme goal of business and that organizational structures should be adapted to that goal. But before discussing performance we must devote some attention to the characteristics of types of enterprises.

Types and Characteristics of European Corporations

European capitalism has assumed a plurality of forms in accordance with its varied history. It is difficult to generalize on the one hand and yet to do justice to the great variety of types which exist. The threefold classification which we present in table 3.5 is therefore something of a mould to be used in focusing on important differences.

Large corporations can be distinguished according to a number of ownership and control variables into an Anglo-Saxon type, a Germanic type and a Latinic one. From the table, the orientation of each type can be quickly deduced.

Anglo-Saxon corporations

Anglo-Saxon corporations are nearly always quoted on the stock exchange, have a broad shareholder base with private and

[80]

Table 3.5 Characteristics of European corporate types

Corporate type	Anglo-Saxon	Germanic	Latinic
		Types of corporations	
Shareholder concentration	–	+	++
Firm networks	–	+	++
Capital market orientation	++	–	–
Market for corporate control	++	–	+
Bank orientation	–	++	+
Employee participation	–	+	–
Autonomy of corporate management	++	+	–

++   important in a general sense
+   of some importance but not in a general way
–   unimportant, not at all or only indirectly influential
Anglo-Saxon firms: those with headquarters in the UK and Ireland
Germanic firms: those with headquarters in Germany, The Netherlands, Scandinavia, Switzerland and Austria
Latinic firms: with headquarters in France, Belgium, Italy, Spain, Portugal, Greece

(financial) institutional owners of shares, who largely evaluate a corporation's management on its financial performance. Management, and especially the chief executive officer or president of the board, is an autonomous figure, who decides on the policy of the firm. Banks are important from a corporate point of view but have no direct interest in the firm; they provide only short- to medium-term finance and do not want to be involved in policy making. Neither is labour, apart from issues of pay and some aspects of social welfare. The verdict on a firm's performance is therefore confined to the capital markets: the evolution of a company's share price is a decisive and 'objective' criterion by which to judge the behaviour of management. If a corporation is profitable and expansionary, its quoted shares on the stock exchange will rise, based on dividend pay-outs and future prospects. If not, the top management is held responsible and gets the blame. A lower share price may be the result of disappointment with current achievements, of reduced expectations and of some sales by investors. This is a sign to management that it should improve the company's performance soon or expect a bid from some other firm to take it over. Such a bid may either be negotiated with the incumbent management or just brought out to shareholders. If the management of the low-priced firm resists the bid, it is called an unfriendly takeover but, obviously, this may be a way of getting a better price for the shares or to gain time in order to organize defensive action, sometimes by calling in a third firm, more attractive to management, sometimes by selling parts of the firm in order to improve the share price and make the bid more costly.

Ostensibly these proceedings are perfectly rational, and the market for corporate control is seen by Anglo-Saxon financial interests as a system keeping an otherwise autonomous management under control, serving the interests of the 'owners' of the corporation: the shareholders. This may be true or not – it is as easy to rationalize actions which may in reality be speculative, and destructive to the corporations's future, if inspired by short-term financial advantage, as it is possible to hold that a corporations's past behaviour was wrong and may be corrected through bids. Controversies about the market for corporate control run high and it would seem that arguments for both sides of the debate sound plausible. Moreover, examples sustaining both positions can easily be found.

The best that can be said is that mergers and takeover bids are an essential element in the Anglo-Saxon system of corporate capitalism. Alongside the annual general meeting where share-holders can voice their opinions with respect to the policies of the management of the corporation and the stock market, where they can sell in case of discontent, the corporate control fights via bids and counter-bids serve to give shareholders a potential leverage over the corporation. We thus arrive at the crucial question: is the running of a corporation in the interest of its shareholders also to the benefit of the other participants and, more generally, does it promote economic welfare for society at large? If firms are small, as in the first half of the nineteenth century, such a question is irrelevant, but with the advent of the big corporation the question should be raised whether the corporate structure serves the common interest and not just that of one of the stakeholders.

Germanic corporations

The structure of the *Germanic corporation* is substantially different from that just discussed. According to table 3.5 these corporate types have a bank orientation, and also have employee influence on their business policies. In addition, there is shareholder direction in the sense that one or a few dominant shareholders (whether as individual persons, families, institutions or other companies, holding important stakes) may exert a preponderant influence. Having such stakes, their holders are naturally inclined to make their views known to the management of the corporation who, in turn, would be ill-advised to neglect such views.

Bank-orientation means one or more of the following: (1) banks may hold shares in the corporation (2) they may have voting power in the general assembly through the deposit voting system, which involves a transfer of votes of (small) individual shareholders to the banks, and (3) banks, who have voting power by means of (1) and (2) may concert their actions to jointly force a solution in case a corporation runs into difficulties. As a result, banks account for over 80 per cent of the voting rights at the

[83]

general meetings of widely held corporations (Kalfass, 1988, p. 782) and may easily concert their voting behaviour with that of dominant stockholders in other cases. Moreover, the shareholdings of banks and insurance companies in non-financial corporations are rising, from 9 per cent in 1960 to 15 per cent in 1980 and 22 per cent in 1990, according to the Bundesbank (1991). Another source, the Monopolkommission (1994, pp. 202–6) documents the important capital stakes which banks, insurance companies (mainly Allianz) and other firms have in the 100 largest German corporations. In other countries, like The Netherlands and Switzerland, the situation is not substantially different, although the forms may diverge from the German situation. The Dutch ING bank has a 5 per cent or larger stake in more than 70 of the 135 stock-exchange quoted firms. Of the 100 largest Dutch companies, many have dominant (family or company) shareholders or are jointly held by a few other firms. A detailed study of the 135 stock-exchange quoted firms came to the conclusion that only four firms could be taken over by means of a bid for their shares (van der Hoeven, 1995, p. 29). A market for corporate control therefore does not exist in Germanic countries (see the survey in de Jong, 1991).

Also, Germanic corporations have labour as an important stakeholder in corporate decision making. I will not review the institutional background here, but stress some essential points for the operation of business corporations. First, the works councils developed more and more from interest groups who defended the social acquirings of employees to an economically active and participative co-management. Labour time models, teamwork, control systems, product policy and sales strategy, as well as cost–price analysis are increasingly discussed at top and lower management levels, and alternative proposals are not shied away from. Second, formal decision-making power still resides in the hands of managers, but the practical effects of rational discussion and consensus formation in the economic domain are

[84]

working through. Several causes promote this: top management becomes more convinced of the usefulness (Henzler, 1994, pp. 114–25); employees are better educated and less ideologically inspired than 20 years ago, when the Works Council Acts came to be adopted: restructuring of operations requires concerted efforts; hierarchies are crumbling; and the practical knowledge and experience of the shopfloor people are taken into account. Third, labour has become a too-expensive factor of production to neglect. Alongside rationalization movements, accompanied by dismissals of people, one notices an effort to involve a better-trained labour force in decision making (Ruess, 1994, no. 13).

Consequently, the management of a Germanic firm makes its decisions less autonomously than an Anglo-Saxon president. Its policies are – depending on the situation and the power distribution – based more on consultancy and consensus with the relevant interest groups.

Latinic corporations

The Latinic corporation (table 3.5) still is marked by large shareholders and some influence of the banks, but also by financial groupings. Shareholders may be private persons or families, led by tycoons, as in Italy's large private firms, or by other companies (in France just over 50 per cent of the owners of large corporations are other corporations), or the state. State enterprise is still an important factor in Spain, Italy and France, in contrast to the Northern EU countries. None of these companies can be acquired by public bids on the capital market. Acquisitions do occur, according to Chevalier (1977, pp. 67–77), Guattri (1993, p. 179) and Morin (1990, pp. 54–71), whenever the performance of a firm leaves something to be desired. Then rival firms appear but they have to persuade active and passive owners that they can do better, and investment bankers like

[85]

Mediobanca, Paribas Suez, and others play an intermediating role. But banks generally do not have long-term stakes. Latinic management, mostly very competent because of its education and training, thus operates under the control and often in the presence of prominent stockholders and their representatives.

However, labour is not recognized as a stakeholder in the corporation, and works councils, if present at all, as in French firms – the *comités d'enterprises*, do not have comparable real power as in Germanic firms (Szarka, 1992, p. 200). Certainly not beyond the social domain, though the *comités* have a lawful right to be informed about the financial accounts. In fact, labour relations in large Latinic corporations have often been antagonistic. But vertical hierarchy, especially in French firms, is paired by lower managers' freedoms and responsibilities in horizontal layers: 'with the end understood, individuals use personal initiative to find the means' (Szarka, 1992, p. 242).

In appearance, the organizational system is highly centralized and strongly concentrated at the top; this prevents outsider influence unless tolerated by the owners. Inside, discretionary decision making can be exercised by managers in their own spheres of influence with little interference from above. This 'dependent individualism' as it is called by Szarka (1993, p. 242) provides for a lot of flexibility and adaptive power.

To summarize: with all the differences and varieties which exist between the various corporate systems, one may distinguish two essential elements, which set Germanic and Latinic types of firms apart from Anglo-Saxon corporations. First, the Continental firms are not subjected to outside control of the capital markets and, second, internal control and decision making occurs in a much less autonomous manner than in Anglo-Saxon types of corporations. Managerial decision making in Continental firms is therefore less one-sided in its orientation and more inclined to take the interests of other stakeholders into account.[8]

[86]

The Current Performance of European Corporations

How to measure the performance of corporations? Four basic standards could be considered, each with their own peculiarities. These would be sales, net surplus value or added value, market capitalization or the value of the firm on the stock exchange, and employment.

Except for the latter, all standards of measurement are influenced by the value of money, both in a temporal and in a regional sense. However, calculations carried out for different years with divergent exchange rates for groups of European corporations show only small deviations in rank-order lists. The outcomes presented below, therefore, are sufficiently robust with respect to monetary changes.

Employment

Employment is an important standard, especially from the point of view of the unions or national governments which face high rates of unemployment. Yet, the standard is treacherous, because big business might improve its overall position by pushing off activities in the vertical chain to other, mainly small, firms who can perform them better. Restructuring, in the sense of selling activities in particular sectors of industry to other, specialized firms, is another occurrence which might reduce employment while improving the firm's position. The same applies to rationalization in the core business, which may be a sign of strength or of weakness (in case of a long-term declining sector). The standard is therefore not unequivocal.

[87]

Sales

Sales is another, often-used standard against which to measure performance. Though easily available and useful for certain purposes, sales or sales per employee is an equally unreliable standard for measuring the performance of large corporations. It neglects aspects such as the degree of vertical integration, capital intensity and sectoral differences, aspects which may bring distortions even within the same sector. In 1993 Degussa, one of the large German chemical firms, had sales per employee of Ecu 232,500; Hoechst and Bayer, the two largest firms in the sector, achieved no more than 139,700 and 139,400 respectively. However, calculation of net value added per employee showed a reverse order: Degussa Ecu 45,200 as against more than Ecu 50,000 for the other two corporations. This is a still more serious problem if we want to compare mixed groups containing, for example, retail, pharmaceutical and steel or motor car corporations.

Market capitalization

Market capitalization is a standard often used to measure the importance of firms in Anglo-Saxon countries. For example, an editorial in one of the *Financial Times* annual lists of the 500 largest European corporations advocates the use of such a standard (*Financial Times*, 1994, p. 3). I disagree. First, the standard is inadequate for measuring non-quoted companies, of which there are many among European large businesses. Consequently, the *Financial Times* list has 187 UK corporations against only 67 German, 77 French, 26 Swiss, 17 Dutch and 22 Swedish corporations, which numbers (and the accompanying market values) distort the relative corporate activity in the various countries.

Second, the standard reflects implicitly the assumption that

[88]

corporate performance to the benefit of shareholders (the maximization of shareholder value) is also in the interest of other stakeholders or of society in general. As such it displays the Anglo-Saxon 'prejudice' that widely held corporations are owned by stockholders. A widespread Continental view would be that such shareholders are the owners of shares, but not of the corporation which, transcending any preponderant interest of individuals or groups, is owned by nobody. Who owns the city of Amsterdam? Obviously nobody, not even large firms, real estate owners or similar people. Yet the corporation exists and is run through decision making.[9]

Economic theory

In view of these criticisms, we will have to rely on economic theory. The question what the performance of a company is, is after all an economic problem. According to economics the existence of a firm is justified when its net output shows a sufficient surplus over and above the purchases made to gain the output. If the conversion is due to labour, capital and the government, who, under the guidance of top management, convert the purchased items into saleable products and services, the conversion ratio should be as high as possible, and in any case should reward those productive services at their market rates. In other words, performance can be measured by the *net added value* brought forward by the combination of production factors; that is also the sum of the rewards for productive contributions. Calculated simply, it is (net) total sales, minus purchases and depreciation. From the point of view of economic theory it is now at once clear that the performance of a firm should not be measured by the remunerations of the capital suppliers or only a part of them (that is, shareholders) but by the totality of the rewards of all those production factors

[89]

which contribute to the final result. To quote the late Sir John Hicks: 'it is not necessarily to the social advantage that control should be tossed about, in pursuit of short-term financial gains' (Hicks, 1983, p. 20). To be sure, this reasoning assumes reasonably competitive markets in both final products and factor inputs, but the discussion of this assumption is irrelevant in the present context because it underlies both the market capitalization and the net value added approaches.

In addition, one could argue that even countries with strong competition policies, such as the US or Germany, do not contest more than a tiny fraction (e.g. in case of mergers less than 0.5 per cent) of potentially dominant positions.

At the University of Amsterdam an investigation has been made since 1991 to measure the hundred largest European corporations according to the net value added (NVA) approach. To achieve comparability the annual reports of those corporations were 'standardized', that is, practices with respect to depreciation (of fixed assets, brands and goodwill), to restructuring funds and the evaluation of assets were harmonized and (if necessary) corrected as if corporations were subjected to the prescriptions of the US GAAP rules and the recommendations of the EU's Thirteenth Guideline were brought into practice.[10] This method of treatment of the accounts of large corporations comes as near as possible to the optimum as a theoretical economist could hope for. The accounting literature also comes to realize that value added is a standard to be preferred to cash flow or dividend per share as a measuring rod (*Belkaoui and Fekrat*, 1994, pp. 3–15).

In tables 3.6, 3.7 and 3.8 both the formation and the distribution of net added value are given for the types of corporations we distinguished above. In the note to table 3.5 it was pointed out which corporations belong to each of the three types of capitalism. In the case of the three Anglo-Dutch corporations – Royal Dutch-Shell, Unilever and Reed Elsevier

[90]

– it was decided to allot them wholly to the Anglo-Saxon domain to add some weight to this group.[11]

The generation of net added value

The formation of surplus value in table 3.6 is based on the 121 corporations which belonged to the group of the hundred largest for at least one of the years 1991–4 (inclusive). As was shown in another publication (de Jong, 1995, p. 409), there is hardly a difference in the results obtained with the group of firms which belonged to the 100 largest in all years. It follows from the left-hand part of table 3.6 that the Germanic group of firms has the largest share of the number and mass of all corporations, and their average size is above average. The Latinic group comes next and the Anglo-Saxon group is the smallest one in respect of the three variables mentioned.

The right-hand part of table 3.6 shows the development of net surplus value throughout the four years. It shows the uneven cyclical developments: the British recession of 1991–2 was followed by an upturn in the following years, and the Continental recession of 1993 was superseded in 1994. Even during so short a period as four years, the increasing weight of the Germanic corporations is visible: the share of this group in the total mass of net added value of European corporations rose from 46.0 per cent to 50.1 per cent; the Anglo-Saxon share fell from 25.1 per cent to 22.2 per cent.[12] In studying the developments during those four years, one gets the impression that two factors account for the shift: first, the typical capitalist reaction of the Anglo-Saxon corporations to the cyclical recession and, second, the influence of the takeover market.

In response to the downturn, the British firms cut down substantially on their labour force – which feel some 16 per cent between 1991 and 1994 – in order to restore or improve their

[91]

profitability. They hardly increased the mass of their net value surplus. In addition, the number of British firms in the group of the largest European corporations did not increase – and so their share fell by three percentage points to 25.8 per cent – because of the takeover market. Some firms were taken over, others were split up, still others disappeared from the lists because growth considerations are not of first importance in Anglo-Saxon capitalism. Continental firms reduced employment by only 2 per cent during the four-year period.

Table 3.6 The formation of net surplus value (averages 1991 through 1994 for those corporations being in the lists of the 100 largest in at least one year)

| Corporations | | *Averages* | | | | |
		1991–94	*1991*	*1992*	*1993*	*1994*
Anglo-Saxon	Number	32	31	31	33	32
	Mass of NVA	98.1	99.6	93.6	98.1	101.1
	Average size	3.1	3.2	3.0	3.0	3.2
Germanic	Number	52	47	51	54	54
	Mass of NVA	204.7	182.8	199.6	207.8	228.3
	Average size	4.0	3.9	3.9	3.8	4.2
Latinic	Number	37	32	39	4.0	38
	Mass of NVA	122.2	114.7	126.5	121.5	126.0
	Average size	3.3	3.6	3.2	3.0	3.3
Total, all European	Number	121	110	121	127	124
	Mass of NVA	425.0	397.1	419.7	427.4	455.4
	Average size	3.5	3.6	3.5	3.4	3.7

Mass of net value added and average size of corporation in billion ECU. Three Anglo-Dutch corporations included in the Anglo-Saxon group. Number of firms rounded off to the nearest integral figure
Source: FEM database

[92]

It is remarkable to see how large Continental firms have surged forward in comparison with the British top group in the long run. In 1965 Britain had 54 corporations with more than $250 million sales each; Germany had 28, France 23 and Italy only eight. Those 54 corporations had total sales of 38.9 billion dollars, produced by 3.4 million employees. The 28 German firms had sales of $24.3 billion, brought forward by 1.9 million employees. It is clear that UK corporations in the large-size class were more numerous than the Continental firms; again, the very largest surpassed their rivals appreciably (de Jong, 1971, p. 66, table 1).

Table 3.7 compares the size ratios during the past 30 years. The relative decline in size of the largest UK firms (industrials only) is a general one and was more pronounced between 1962–71 and 1981–93 than in the intermediate period. Both decades were marked by strong merger and takeover booms of which the UK had a more than proportionate share. One of the first contested bids was that by ICI for Courtaulds in 1962, soon followed by several others, especially during the 1980s. In view of the fact that the overall UK economy grew somewhat faster than the economies of most other EU countries during the 1980s, the negative influence of the takeover market on corporate growth seems plausible.

Comparative productivity

At first sight the last sentence of the previous paragraph may seem to contradict the findings of table 3.7. If merger and takeover activity of the firms of a particular country is strong in comparison with that of the corporations of other countries will they not gain in relative importance? However, this is not a foregone conclusion. If merger and takeover activity does not improve productivity (i.e. total net value added divided by

[93]

Table 3.7 Size ratios of UK and Continental
large corporations

Size class	1962	1971	1981	1993	1994[a]
1–5	2.35	1.55	1.72	0.91	0.97
6–10	0.84	0.78	0.46	0.35	0.48
11–20	0.64	0.54	0.45	0.31	0.43
21–30	0.68	0.46	0.46	0.34	0.34

[a] Also included are non-industrial corporations in banking, insurance, transport, retailing, etc.; see *Fortune* (1995).
Sources: Jacquemin and de Jong (1977, p. 101) and calculations

employees) but is undertaken to increase financial results or, in other words, to raise the share of stockholders in the net value added achieved, mergers and takeovers may well hamper the growth of corporations or, at best, have a neutral impact on such growth. Thus there are two aspects to this question of corporate growth: value productivity and value distribution.

The latter aspect will be taken up in the next paragraph, so let us concentrate here on the productivity question. In table 3.8, the first three columns repeat the findings of table 3.6, whereas columns four and five provide a measure of comparative productivity. Net value added per employee (NVA/E) eliminates the influence of the size and degree of vertical integration of the corporations which are compared. The measurement by means of the percentage of firms which have a NVA/E above the European median (which was 42,000 ECU on average throughout the period 1991–4) eliminates a possible disturbing influence from a small group of very highly productive firms on the overall averages for the three types of corporations. Such distortions might occur if the sectoral compositions of the corporations from the three types of domains would diverge strongly. In fact, oil, gas and energy firms, telecom companies, pharmaceutical and media corporations have a substantially higher value–productivity than firms from other sectors; however, the number of such firms in comparison with the total number for the three domains did not diverge: the Anglo-Saxon share was 30 per cent, like the Latinic share, and the Germanic share 26 per cent.

On the other hand, firms in retail distribution and companies producing steel, glass and non-ferrous metals have a much lower value productivity than average, but again their shares in the total number of firms per domain did not diverge: 17–18 per cent. Therefore, the sectoral representation of the corporations in each of the three domains is not a disturbing factor.

The results from table 3.8 justify the conclusion that the value productivity of Anglo-Saxon firms is below the European

Table 3.8 Dimensions and productivity of European corporations (averages for the years 1991–94)

Corporations	Number of corporations	Total value added	Size per firm	NVA/E	% above median
Anglo-Saxon	32	98.1	3.1	41.7	35.3
Germanic	52	204.7	4.0	48.3	56.8
Latinic	37	122.2	3.3	46.0	53.2
Total, all European	121	425.0	3.5	45.9	50.1

Royal Dutch-Shell, Unilever and Reed Elsevier included in the Anglo-Saxon group
Value added in billion ECU; size of firm in billion ECU
Net value added per employee (NVA/E) in thousand ECU
Medians calculated per annum; average median size 42,000 ECU
Source: FEM data base

average. Both measurements employed – columns 4 and 5 – registrate the outcomes for a number of years in which all countries went through recession and revival.

It should also be remarked that firm or sector capital-intensity differences do not influence importantly the measurements, because we have calculated net value added figures, that is, gross value added minus depreciation, and the depreciation rates have been adapted to sector requirements and standardized throughout the European population of firms.

If our results achieved do indicate that Anglo-Saxon productivity is generally below the European average, the relative lagging of Anglo-Saxon corporations, such as was demonstrated in table 3.7, can be plausibly explained. A productivity differential of, say 10–15 per cent each year for a succession of decades undermines the basis of existence of a good proportion of once-reputable firms. No amount of corporate takeover activity can compensate for that.

The Distribution of Net Added Value

Table 3.9 instructs us about the division of the surplus product over the three groups of labour, capital suppliers and the government. This table restricts the population of firms to the core of the 100 largest for each year, and averages the shares of the three stakeholder groups over the four years 1991–4. This approach was chosen because the distributional data were readily available for the 100 largest corporations per annum, and the additional firms, moving into and out of the lists every year (as in table 3.6) would have had to be inserted separately – a cumbersome procedure.

It follows from table 3.9 that there is a substantial difference between Anglo-Saxon firms and Continental ones. The first group pays out a much smaller share to labour (varying between

69.9 per cent in 1992 to 60.2 per cent in 1994), and higher shares to capital suppliers and the government (in taxes). The Continental firms have, on average, shares of 80 per cent to labour, and something like half the rates of the British firms paid to capital suppliers and the government.

However, inside the Continental groups there are important differences, with German firms having labour shares of over 85 per cent in all years, French firms over 80 per cent and Swiss, Scandinavian and Dutch firms some 75 per cent or over. It is the latter groups – especially the Swiss and Dutch ones – who also have the highest retention rates, i.e. the shares saved by the corporations themselves, namely 8.7 per cent as against 3.2 per cent and 3.4 per cent for the British and German ones.[13] The 2

Table 3.9 The distribution of net surplus value
Core group of 82 largest corporations; averages for
1991–4, in percent of total net added value

Number	Corporations	Labour	Capital	Government	Retained shares	Dividends paid
22	Anglo-Saxon	62.2	23.5	14.3	3.2	15.0
35	Germanic	86.1	8.8	5.1	5.2	3.0
25	Latinic	80.3	14.4	5.3	3.0	4.7
82	Total European (averages[a])	79.0	13.7	7.3	3.6	6.1

[a] The figures on this line are not the average of the three groups because their weights diverge

Dividends and retained shares do not equal the capital supplier's share because net interest payments and third-party shares were left out. The core group consists of firms, registered in the top 100 per year with at least three years of comparable figures.

Source: Constructed from the FEM database, 1991 through 1994

per cent difference in the retention rates between the Anglo-Saxon and the Germanic corporations does not seem to be much of a difference but, in view of the much larger mass of net added value of the latter group (table 3.6) it amounts to over 4 billion ECU, on average, per year. This means that Germanic corporations have larger reserves to finance their expansion (and notwithstanding their heavy depreciation, see above), than the companies belonging to both other domains. The most striking difference is the share paid out to shareholders in dividends. The British firms pay a stunning 15.0 per cent of their net added value to shareholders, some three to four times as much as their Continental counterparts. This tendency to maximize shareholder value is visible throughout the group of the 32 Anglo-Saxon firms, with the exception only of a few corporations – mostly those in financial troubles. If anything, these figures highlight the structurally different organization of the respective types of firms, mentioned in lines 3 and 4 of table 3.5.

Distributional Effects

The distribution of net added value in favour of capital suppliers is, of course, an institutional fact, but it has some important consequences.

1 There will be a systematic under-investment in the labour force, which, however, in the currently large corporation, and more so in future ones, must be considered to be the most potent resource for generating future surplus values. With the increasing knowledge intensity of business, investments in employee training, team responsibility and devotion to the goals of the firm should be considered of the utmost importance. When the interest of the capital suppliers takes overriding importance, such investments

tend to be underrated and neglected. The formation of surplus value takes second seat behind the distributional aspects, hurting long-run performance.

2　The high dividend percentages are only sustainable under the regime of an unfettered market for corporate control. The constant threat of being dismissed by a takeover prompts management to take protective measures: exorbitant salaries, stock options, golden handshakes, exaggerated pension provisions, etc. are some of the precautionary measures to ensure against takeover events. Because such high management compensations are a general phenomenon, whereas the chance of being taken over is restricted, this is a costly system, after all: it contains substantial amounts of rents, paid for the bearing of uncertainty which is not linked to the generation of surplus values, but immanent in the system itself. In addition, it promotes similar attitudes with employees or may demotivate them.

It is small wonder that Anglo-Saxon literature is replete with discussions about shirking, opportunistic behaviour, risk avoidance and moral hazard (for a devastating critique of such mental patterns, see Hampden-Turner and Trompenaars, 1993). In other words, it is structure of the system which orients human behaviour and not the other way round.

3　The substantial sums paid out to shareholders reduce the finance available for growth and the attainment of critical mass. Now, whereas size *per se* is not a good thing to strive for, a globalizing economy offers many opportunities in distant places for which a certain minimum size is necessary in order to be able to play the game at all. If the managers of the Dutch East India Company had responded to the repeated complaints of shareholders, the company would never have been able to expand and survive for the next two centuries the way it did. The figures presented in table 3.7

[99]

demonstrate that this is still a pertinent consideration in present times.

4   As against the preceding arguments it might be held that shareholders, receiving the high dividends, can invest these sums in innovative ventures which open up new lines of business. Apart from the fact that existing large corporations can start new businesses too (for example, by means of joint ventures), it is true that many new ventures arise from small entrepreneurial initiatives, financed by an agile and well-developed capital market. There are many indications that Anglo-Saxon countries have an advantage in this respect *vis à vis* Continental countries. However, large Continental firms can and do buy up such firms, in which case they must pay the entrepreneurial rents. Whether this is worthwhile depends on the length of the innovation cycles and the aptness of the corporate acquisition policies.

5   Another remark relates to the contribution by corporations to government revenue which, according to table 3.9, is more than double the share in net value added in Anglo-Saxon corporations in comparison with Continental ones. As the corporate profit tax in Britain is generally lower, this higher share seems due to the higher gross profit level. In any case, for a given amount of net value generated, Anglo-Saxon firms seem to contribute more to the general welfare, but such a conclusion may be premature. A good deal of British welfare expenditure is paid out of government revenues, whereas Continental welfare provisions are largely financed from premiums paid by employers and employees which are grouped as part of the labour share. So, to this extent, the differences are overstated.

6   A curious result of the capital market orientation in recent years is the *hara-kiri* mentality of Anglo-Saxon firms which seems to be developing. Large corporations are splitting themselves up into separately quoted firms – ICI, British

Gas, Hanson, Boots, etc. – or are said to have plans to do so (Thorn-Emi). Whereas the specific reasons advanced for such behaviour differ in each individual case, the common argument seems to be the financial synergy which is said to be attainable: the parts, taken separately, achieve greater market value than the previous whole. In all of these cases, the firms concerned showed a bad performance in terms of the growth of net value added; if the initial year (1991) is put at 100, subsequent years remained below that level.[14] Thus, by dividing themselves in response to a lacklustre industrial performance, the owners apparently hope to cash the benefits from independent existence or sale. This provides opportunities for rich Continental corporations (Rover, Boots Pharmaceuticals, merchant banks, etc.). This phenomenon also contributes to the slow but inexorable Germanization of the European corporate landscape (table 3.6).

Corporations and Capital Markets

The share of capital in the net added value of British large firms was found to be markedly higher than with Continental firms in the earlier-mentioned article (de Jong, 1995). So was their profitability, measured as net return on sales or as return on capital employed (de Jong, 1991, pp. 11–13). This raises the question: how it is possible that international capital markets and especially the large institutional investors operating there, tolerate such discrepancies? The answer may be provided by table 3.10 comparing the two standards for groups of the 20 largest British and Continental corporations. It will be seen that the British group had a lower NAV per employee (but somewhat less pronounced than in table 3.8 because the group included relatively more highly productive British firms). In 1993 the

[101]

market value of the British group was 3.1 times higher than that of the Continental group. The share of capital in NAV was 19 per cent in the British case as against only 4.3 per cent in the Continental group of firms. The ratios market value/net added value and rate of return (as a percentage) follow from the first three columns.

However, because 1993 was a cyclically better year for the British firms than for the Continentals, I have compared the same B:A quotients for 1991 – a year in which the cycle favoured the Continental firms. It will be seen at once that the ratio market value/net added value and the rate of return ratio hardly differs for the two years.

Table 3.10 A comparison of added value and market value of leading British and Continental firms (1993)

	Net added value (1)	Market value (2)	Share of capital (3)	Market value/ added value (2):(1)	Rate of return in % (1).(3) (2)
A The 20 largest Continental firms	43,5	59,0	4,3	1,4	3,2
B The 20 largest British firms	39,7	184,000	19,0	4,6	4,1
B:A in 1993	0,91	3,1	4,4	3,3	1,3
B:A in 1991	0,84	2,8	2,3	3,3	0,7

Net added value in thousand Ecu per employee; market value is company's stock market capitalization in 1,000 Ecu per employee early in September of the years mentioned; capital share as a percentage of net added value
Sources: The hundred largest European companies according to net value from *Financieel-Economisch* magazine, November 1992 and November 1994. Market capitalization derived from *Financial Times.* Europe's Top 500 companies by market capitalization, January 1992 and January 1994

It can be deduced from table 3.10, therefore, that it is the much higher share of capital in the distribution of net added value in the British case which is responsible for the three times higher level of market value (column 2). Thus the distribution of the surplus value generated determines corporate market values. Investors are not interested in buying Continental stock which is low priced because they cannot change the capital share in the net added value of those Continental firms. If they bought, they would only drive down the rate of return on such investments in comparison with British rates of return. On the other hand, selling British stock would depress market values and raise British rates of return to a structurally higher level than Continental companies' rates. International capital markets therefore have equalized those rates of return already; they deviate only slightly from a 1:1 relationship (as in 1991 and 1993) because of cyclical circumstances.

A substantial change in the market values of both groups of corporations would only be brought about, it seems, if either of the groups would alter appreciably the share of capital in net value added (table 10.3, column 3). But this can hardly be expected. If the British reduced that share (say to some 11 per cent, the overall average for the majority of the Continental firms in the group of the 100 largest European firms) their market values would collapse, with disastrous consequences for institutional and private investors. Thus British firms are unable to adopt a Continental institutional regime, even if they were willing to do so.

In reverse, Continental firms would have to dismantle their institutional regimes, that is rob the banks and dominant shareholders of their possessions and deny labour its acquired legal rights. But why should Continental firms be inclined to pay out higher capital shares? Such a course would hurt their productivity and growth, which are at present higher. In view of these considerations I do not think that the so-called

[103]

convergence thesis (Moerland, 1995) is convincing.

In addition, the large Continental firms are not in need of the finance provided by international capital markets. Most of the financial means, needed for growth (70–100 per cent, depending on the circumstances) comes from retentions and heavy depreciation. The latter were corrected in the net value added tables above, in accordance with the standardized procedures to calculate net value added. But obviously these sums are available to the firms concerned. Such corrections diverge substantially as between the corporations of different countries. British annual reporting is usually truthful and the corrections were therefore slight: 0.77 per cent of total net value added. This was also applicable to the French corporations (0.64 per cent). But in the case of the other Continental corporations, and especially the Germanic ones, the corrections were, at nearly 3 per cent higher.

Gross depreciation rates (gross added value minus net value as a percentage of the first) varied between 24.6 per cent (French firms), 25.6 per cent (British firms) and 27.5 per cent (Germanic corporations). Therefore, these 2–3 per cent differences, plus the higher corrections, as well as the 2 per cent difference in the retention rates mentioned earlier (see the section on the distribution of surplus value above) add up to something like 5 per cent of the total mass of NAV which is some 10 billion ECU per annum on average. Suppose these large corporations have an average growth rate of 5 per cent and an average capital–output ratio of 1, the flow of funds should be sufficient to finance expansion without recourse to the capital market.[15]

French firms are used to finance coming from families, other linked corporations (including financial ones) and the state. The latter source is drying up, so privatizations have opened the road to the capital market. However, it is Anglo-Saxon firms who are most in need of such a market, but some of the most important among them visit the place only when it suits their purposes. The so-called 'disciplinary' role of capital markets should be taken

[104]

with a grain of salt: it is mainly a feature to be found in financial textbooks and papers which advocate this role for ideological reasons (see *The Economist*, 1996).

Grasshoppers or Ants?

European corporations have shown a variety of structures and a different performance in the course of time. No firm has been able to achieve an unbroken record of good performance and that is naturally not to be expected in an uncertain and changing world. Moreover, there seems to be a great diversity of organizations and strategies which lead to success or failure, depending strongly on the institutional, sectoral and personal preconditions necessary for the realization of these results. Nevertheless, one contrast seems to be relevant to all times and places: the grasshopper makes dazzling jumps and appears more brilliant than the ants, who industriously and co-operatively build their ant-hills. For a time the former (whether they be Daimler-Benz, Metallgesellschaft, Hanson or Ferruzi) seem to outperform the latter, but sooner or later the jumps are found to have been not so glorious. In the corporate world, it is the ants who endure and an institutional structure should be conducive to ant-like behaviour.

Notes

1 This differentiating term appears already in the fourteenth century (see Origo, 1963, p. 111); it has been annexed by lawgivers to describe a company's legal structure. But economic practice has its own ways.
2 North and Thomas (1973, p. 155): 'By 1700 the institutional framework of England provided a hospitable environment for

growth'; e.g., 'Between 1688 and 1695 the number of joint-stock companies increased from 22 to 150'.

3 Gaastra (1991, pp. 86–7). Without the military, the number was still between 14,000 and 25,000.

4 See den Heyer (1994, pp. 119–22), Gøbel, in De Bruyn and Gaastra (1993, pp. 106–8) and Chaudhuri in the same volume (pp. 50–5). The British East India Company was less vertically integrated, not building their own ships. After the merger between the Hudson Bay Company and North West Company in 1821, the HBC employed 1,983 men. See Newman (1987, p. 298).

5 Clapham in Taylor (1958, p. 22). The firms were Monteith, Bogle and Co. from Glasgow and Horrocks, Miller and Co. from Preston, both in 1816.

6 Farnie (1979, p. 269).

7 Milward and Saul (1973, p. 93), at the end of the eighteenth century.

8 Henzler (1994, pp. 114–25) remarks: 'There is . . . the imperative need to inform, convince and motivate a large number of stakeholders of widely varying origins'. Henzler is president of the McKinsey organization in Germany.

9 The problem was raised long ago in an interesting volume edited by Hacker (1965, pp. 3–5), in which the ultimate – a corporation without employees or stockholders, that is a fully automated business owning its own shares – is achieved and run by a committee of ten managers. The consequences are traced in an amusing interchange during a senatorial investigation.

10 The data and procedures followed are annually published in the Dutch *Financieel-Economisch* (Financial and Economic) *Magazine*. See *FEM* of November 1992, 1993, 1994, 1995.

11 This trite reason was invoked in order to avoid lengthy discussions about their 'true character'. The addition to the British group was substantial in the four years considered, namely one-fifth of the mass mentioned in table 3.6.

12 The percentage shifts were about the same if the corporations who were on the lists in all years were taken as a base.

13 This is partly due to the composition of the group of firms considered in the various countries; e.g. the German group comprises no oil and telecom firms, who have high retention rates.

14 This is not necessarily linked to diversified corporations. For example, BTR and BAT Industries improved their net value added by over 30 per cent in just four years.

15 On top of this, the high labour shares in the German distribution of NAV also cover pension reserve dotations, which according to the Bundesbank (October 1991, 22 ff.) were sufficient to finance new equity issues of business during the 1980s. Such dotations have a reinsurance obligation.

References

Baums, Th. (1993): Banks and Corporate Control in Germany. In McCahery, Piciotto and Scott (eds), *Corporate Control and Accountability*, Oxford: Clarendon Press.

——, Buxbaum, R. M. and Hopt, K. J. (eds), (1994): *Institutional Investors and Corporate Governance* (Berlin/New York).

Belkaoui, A. R. and Fekrat, M. A., *The magic in value added: merits of derived accounting indicator numbers*. Managerial Finance, vol. 20, no. 9, pp. 3–15.

Bösselmann, K. (1939): *Die Entwicklung des deutschen Aktienwesens in 19 Jahrhundert*. Berlin: W. de Gruyter & Co.

Bruyn, J. E. and Gaastra, F. S. (eds), (1993): *Ships, Sailors and Spices. East India Companies and their Shipping in the 16th, 17th and 18th Centuries*. Amsterdam: NEHA series III, 20.

Bundesbank, Die Deutsche (1991): *Monatsbericht*. Frankfurt a. Main (October).

Chandler, A. D. (1977): *The Visible Hand: The Managerial Revolution in American Business*. Cambridge, MA: Harvard University Press.

—— and Daems, H. (eds), (1980): *Managerial Hierarchies. Comparative Perspectives on the Rise of the Modern Industrial Enterprise*. Cambridge, MA: Harvard University Press.

Channon, D. F.: (1974): *The Strategy and Structure of British Enterprise*. London and Basingstoke: Macmillan.

Chaudhuri, K. N. (1993): The English East India Company's shipping (c.1660–1760). In Bruyn and Gaastra, *Ships, Sailors and Spices*.

Amsterdam: NEHA series III, 20.

Chevalier, J. M. (1977): *L'Économie Industrielle en Question*. Paris: Calmann-Lévy.

Clapham, J. H. (1966): *The Economic Development of France and Germany, 1815–1914*. 4th edn. Cambridge: Cambridge University Press.

Dyas, G. P. (1972): *The Strategy and Structure of French Industrial Enterprises*. Cambridge, MA: Harvard University Press.

—— and Thanheiser, J. (1976): *The Emerging European Enterprise: Strategy and Structure in French and German Industry*. Colorado: Boulder.

Economist, The (1996): 10 February.

Farnie, D. A. (1979): *The English Cotton Industry and the World Market 1815–1896*. Oxford: Clarendon Press.

Financieel-Economisch Magazine, Amsterdam: *Data base of the hundred largest European corporations*, November 1991, November 1992, November 1993 and October 1994.

Financial Times (1994): January, p. 30.

Fortune (1995): 7 August.

Freedeman, C. E. (1979): *Joint-stock Enterprise in France 1807–1867*. Chapel Hill: University of North Carolina Press.

Guattri, L. (1993): Caratteristiche e tendenze delle imprese in diversi contesti capitalistici. In *Le strutture del capitalismo e l'impresa nella società contemporanea*, Milan: Cariplo, Serie Relazioni, pp. 167–85.

Hacker, A. (ed.), (1965): The Corporation Takeover. *Anchor Books*. New York: Doubleday.

Hampden-Turner, Ch. and Trompenaars, A., 1993: *The Seven Cultures of Capitalism*. New York: Doubleday.

Hannah, L. (1983): *The Rise of the Corporate Economy*. 2nd edn. London and New York: Methuen.

—— (1995): The Joint-stock Company; Concentration and the State 1894–1994. In Allan, A. (ed.), *Proceedings of the Annual Conference 1994*. London: Business Archives Council.

Harbutt-Dawson, W. (1912): Industrial Germany. *The Nation's Library*. London and Glasgow: Collins.

Henzler, H. A. (1994): *Europreneurs. The Men who are shaping Europe*. London: Bantam.

Heyer, H. den (1994): *De Geschiedenis van de West-Indische Compagnie*. Zutphen: Walburg Pers.

Hicks, J. (1983): Limited liability: the pros and cons. In Orhnial, F. (ed.), *Limited Liability and the Corporation*. London and Canberra: Croom Helm.

Hoeven, B. van der (1995): Beschermingsconstructies Nederlandse Beursfondsen. In *Fusies & Overnames*, January/February, pp. 23–30.

Hohenberg, P. (1967): *Chemicals in Western Europe, 1850–1914*. Chicago: Rand McNally.

Israel, J. T. (1989): *Dutch Primacy in World Trade, 1585–1740*, New York, NY: Oxford University Press.

Jacquemin, A. P. and de Jong, H. W. (1977): *European Industrial Organization*. London and Basingstoke: Macmillan.

Jong, H. W. de (1971): *Ondernemingsconcentratie. De Ontwikkelingen in Europa, Amerika en Japan*. Leiden: Stenfert Kroese.

—— (1991): The takeover market in Europe: control structures and the performance of large companies compared. In *Review of Industrial Organization*, vol. 6, no. 1.

—— (ed.), (1993): *The Structure of European Industry*, 3rd edn., Dordrecht/ Boston/London: Kluwer Academic Publishers.

—— (1995): European capitalism: between freedom and social justice. In *Review of Industrial Organization*, vol. 10, no. 4.

—— (1996): Der Markt fuer Unternehmen; Systemverschiedenheiten, Unternehmensleistungen und das Wettbewerbliche Harmonisierungsbedürfnis aus europäischer Sicht. In Kruse and Mayer (eds), *Aktuelle Probleme der Wettbewerbs- und Wirtschaftspolitik*. Baden-Baden: Erhard Kantzenbach zum 65. Geburtstag. Nomos Verlagsgesellschaft.

Kalfass, H. H. (1988): The German experience with stockholder voting. In *Columbia Business Law Review*, no. 3.

Kedar, B. Z. (1976): *Merchants in Crises. Genoese and Venetian Men of Affairs and the Fourteenth Century Depression*. New Haven and London: Yale University Press.

Kellenbenz, H. (1977 and 1981): *Deutsche Wirtschaftsgeschichte*. Munich: Band I u II, Verlag C. H. Beck.

Klepper, S. and Graddy, E. (1990): The evolution of new industries and the determinants of market structure. In *The Rand Journal of Economics*, vol. 21, no. 1.

Landes, D. S. (1969): *The Unbound Prometheus. Technological Change and*

Economic Development in Western Europe from 1750 to the present. Cambridge: Cambridge University Press.

Lane, F. C. and Riemersma, J. C. (eds), (1953): Enterprise and secular change. Section one. Business units. In *Readings in Economic History.* London: George Allen and Unwin.

Managerial Finance (1994): pp. 3–15.

Milward, A. S. and Saul, S. B. (1973): *The Economic Development of Continental Europe.* London: George Allen & Unwin.

Miyashita, K. and Russell, D. (1996): *Keiretsu: Inside the hidden Japanese conglomerates.* New York, NY: McGraw-Hill.

Moerland, P. W. (1995): Corporate ownership and control structures: an international comparison. In *Review of Industrial Organization,* vol. 10, no. 4.

Monopolkommission (1976); Hauptgutachten (1973/1975): *Mehr Wettlewerb ist möglich.* Baden-Baden: Nomos Verlag.

—— (1994): Hauptgutachten 1992/1993, Mehr Wettbewerb auf allen Märkten. Baden-Baden: Nomos Verlag.

Morin, F. (1975): *La Structure Financière du Capitalisme Français.* Paris: Calmann-Lévy.

—— (1990): Qui possède les 200 premières enterprises Françaises? *Science et Vie: Economie,* 63 (Juillet–Août).

Newman, P. C. (1986–8): *Company of Adventurers,* vols. I–III, Hardmondsworth: Penguin Books.

North, D. C. and Thomas, R. P. (1973): *The Rise of the Western World.* Cambridge: Cambridge University Press.

Origo, I. (1963): *The Merchant of Prato. Francesco di Marco Datini.* Hardmondsworth: Penguin Books (first published 1957).

Pavan, R. D. J. (1972): *The Strategy and Structure of Italian Enterprise.* Cambridge, MA: Harvard University Press.

Posthumus, N. W. (1953): *De Oosterse Handel te Amsterdam.* Leiden: E. J. Brill.

Prais, S. J. (1976): *The evolution of giant firms in Britain. A study of the growth of concentration in manufacturing industry in Britain, 1909–1970.* Cambridge: Cambridge University Press.

Roover, R. de (1942): The commercial revolution of the thirteenth century. In Lane, F. C. and Riemersma, J. C. (1953), *Enterprise and Secular Change.*

—— (1966): *The Rise and Decline of the Medici Bank 1397–1494*. New York: Norton (first published 1963).

—— (1974): *Business, Banking and Economic Thought in Late Medieval and Early Modern Europe*. Selected studies of Raymond de Roover., (ed.) J. Kirschner, Chicago/London: University of Chicago Press.

Ruess, A. (1994): Betriebsräte, Anderes Gewicht. *Wirtschaftswoche*, nos. 13/25 (March).

Steensgaard, N. (1982): The Dutch East India Company as an institutional innovation. In Aymard, M. (ed.), *Dutch Capitalism and World Capitalism*. Cambridge: Cambridge University Press.

Szarka, J. (1992): *Business in France. An Introduction to the Economic and Social Context*. London: Pitman.

Taylor, P. A. M. (ed.), (1991): *The industrial revolution in Britain. Triumph or disaster?* Boston: D. C. Heath.

Teece, D. J. (1991): Reconceptualising the corporation and competition. In Faulhaber, G. R. and Tamburini, G. (eds), *European Economic Integration. The role of Technology*. Boston/London/Dordrecht: Kluwer Academic Publishers.

Index

[112]